Extraordinary Faith
For Ordinary Time

Extraordinary Faith For Ordinary Time

Sermons For Pentecost
(Last Third)
Cycle C Gospel Texts

Larry R. Kalajainen

CSS Publishing Company, Inc.
Lima, Ohio

EXTRAORDINARY FAITH FOR ORDINARY TIME

Copyright © 1994 by
The CSS Publishing Company, Inc.
Lima, Ohio

All rights reserved. No part of this publication may be reproduced, stored in a retrieval system, or transmitted in any form or by any means, electronic, mechanical, photocopying, recording, or otherwise, without the prior permission of the publisher. Inquiries should be addressed to: The CSS Publishing Company, Inc., 517 South Main Street, P.O. Box 4503, Lima, Ohio 45802-4503.

Scripture quotations are from the *New Revised Standard Version of the Bible,* copyright 1989 by the Division of Christian Education of the National Council of the Churches of Christ in the USA. Used by permission.

Library of Congress Cataloging-in-Publication Data

Kalajainen, Larry R.
    Extraordinary faith for ordinary time : sermons for Pentecost (last third) Gospel lesson, cycle C / Larry R. Kalajainen.
       p.   cm.
    ISBN 0-7880-0020-9
    1. Pentecost season—Sermons. 2. Bible. N.T. Gospels—Sermons. 3. Sermons, American. I. Title.
BV4300.5.K365   1994
252'.6—dc20   94-1000
                                                                                     CIP

This book is available in the following formats, listed by ISBN:
0-7880-0020-9 Book
0-7880-0021-7 IBM (3 1/2 and 5 1/4) computer disk
0-7880-0022-5 IBM book and disk package
0-7880-0023-3 Macintosh computer disk
0-7880-0024-1 Macintosh book and disk package

Many preachers receive valuable critiques of their sermons after *they have been preached. I am blessed with a partner who has read and offered constructive criticism of every sermon* before *it has been delivered from the pulpit. For all the Saturday morning hours she has spent reading and offering the perspective of the person in the pew, I dedicate this volume to my wife Carol with gratitude.*

Table Of Contents

Introduction	9

Proper 23
Pentecost 21
Ordinary Time 28
    The Saving Power Of Gratitude
    Luke 17:11-19
	13

Proper 24
Pentecost 22
Ordinary Time 29
    Tough Faith In Tough Times
    Luke 18:1-8 (C, RC)
    Luke 18:1-8a (L)
	21

Proper 25
Pentecost 23
Ordinary Time 30
    The Good, The Bad And The Justified
    Luke 18:9-14
	27

Proper 26
Pentecost 24
Ordinary Time 31
    Out On A Limb
    Luke 19:1-10
	35

Reformation Sunday
    The Son Makes Us Free
    John 8:31-36
	43

All Saints' Sunday
    The Politics Of The Saints
    Luke 6:20-31 (C)
	51

All Saints' Sunday   59
    Remembering The Saints
    Matthew 5:1-12 (L, RC)

Proper 27   67
Pentecost 25
Ordinary Time 32
    The Importance Of Asking The Right Questions
    Luke 20:27-38

Proper 28   75
Pentecost 26
Ordinary Time 33
    Not Yet Quitting Time
    Luke 21:5-19

Pentecost 27   83
    Investing God's Gift
    Luke 19:11-27

Thanksgiving Day   93
    The Bread That Endures
    John 6:25-35 (C)
    Luke 17:11-19 (L, RC)

Christ The King   99
    Pleased To Reconcile
    Luke 23:33-43 (C)
    Luke 23:35-43 (L, RC)

Lectionary Preaching After Pentecost   101

C — Revised Common Lectionary; L — Lutheran Lectionary; RC — Roman Catholic Lectionary

Introduction

On December 31, thousands of people will gather in Times Square in New York City to watch the big red apple, symbol of that exciting and turbulent metropolis, descend slowly down the pole atop of which it sits precisely at the stroke of midnight. Millions more will watch the annual ritual on television. Horns will blow, the crowds will cheer, many will embrace and kiss their partners, throw confetti, or toast one another with champagne. A new year will elbow its way onstage, though apart from the change of the calendar, the minute after midnight will differ in no observable way from the minute before midnight. Yet everything will have changed. The old year will be gone forever. It will hold no more possibilities. It is used-up time — past time. The future looms ahead, dark, mysterious, yet full of promise.

However, for Christians, the new year will have already begun some five weeks earlier on the first Sunday in Advent. The observances marking the passing of the old year and the onset of the new will have been markedly different. In contrast to the noisy and boisterous New Year's parties that mark the turning of the calendar, Christians will celebrate their New Year by lighting Advent candles, singing hymns, and offering prayers.

These differences of observance are more significant than they might at first appear. For Christians, the liturgical calendar is not simply a different way of measuring time; it signifies a different way of living in time. Christians measure time, not by months or days or years, but by seasons of the gospel. The yearly commemoration of the birth, life, ministry, death, and resurrection of Jesus are the mileposts that define the quality of time for us. The great gospel events fill time with meaning; they mark time as not merely *chronos* — the passage of time — but as *kairos* — the fullness of time or the opportune time.

The gospel seasons are named for their relationship to the great feasts of Christ's nativity, his passion, and his resurrection. Advent, Christmas, Epiphany, Lent, Holy Week, Easter, and Pentecost are the drumbeats that march us through the days, teaching us to keep time to gospel rhythms.

But the celebration of these gospel feasts does not occupy the whole year. Between Epiphany and Lent are some weeks that have no name. Trinity Sunday leads ... where? A long succession of unnamed weeks stretches ahead until Christ the King Sunday finally brings the liturgical year to its close. These Sundays, which are not related to any of the gospel feasts, are designated "Ordinary Time."

Ordinary time sounds as though it might mean insignificant time. Time when nothing important is happening. Time like any other time. Time that does not demand any particular way of living. Time that is not invested with eternity.

But nothing could be further from the truth. All of time is now sacred time because of the mighty acts of God in Jesus Christ which the major feasts celebrate. We are ordinary people, and ordinary time is a gift to us. It offers us opportunity to practice living by the grace notes of the gospel seasons. It is time filled, not with meanings assigned to it by the gospel events, but with the meanings that we give to it as we live in time as Christ's disciples. God has invested time with meaning, and we celebrate that meaning in the gospel seasons. But we also have an investment to make in time. Ordinary time is our time. It is ours to fill with meaning, with purpose, with faithful discipleship, with love. It is our time to respond to God's revelation and redemption in Christ. It is we who make ordinary time holy. If these sermons for the last third of the church year can help you discover the faith to live an extraordinary life in ordinary time, they will have fulfilled their purpose.

Larry R. Kalajainen
Paris, France

Proper 23
Pentecost 21
Ordinary Time 28
Luke 17:11-19

The Saving Power Of Gratitude

On the old television show "All In The Family," there was an episode when Archie Bunker's son-in-law Mike, or "Meathead" as Archie always called him, asks Archie a riddle. "A young man is seriously injured in an accident and is rushed to the hospital for emergency surgery. When the surgeon is called, it turned out that the young man was the son of the surgeon, but the surgeon was not the boy's father." Archie suggests that the boy was adopted, or that the surgeon was his step-father. But with a triumphant glint in his eye, Mike informs Archie that the surgeon was the boy's mother. Good old Archie, the archetypal male chauvinist, would never have seen the answer to that one. His presuppositions blinded him to the obvious.

The prophet Micah, many centuries ago, proclaimed some obvious, but unpleasant realities to people who were likewise blinded to the truth of their situation by their suppositions. They were solid, middle-class citizens of Jerusalem, morally upright, religious, and socially respectable. They thought God was in their camp, and that their prosperity was the sign of God's favor. But Micah told them otherwise. Their prosperity, he told them, was the result of their having coveted their poorer and weaker neighbors' fields and houses. They seized what they wanted, enriching themselves at the expense of those weaker. But God, who sees what proud and greedy human beings do not, stands over against such pride and power, and takes the part of the weak and the poor. God's judgment is not based on human standards, but on God's own truth and righteousness, and God makes it clear that oppression and exploitation will bear its own bitter fruit.

The people, of course, do not want to hear this message of the prophet. "Don't preach this way," they tell him, "One should not preach this way; disgrace will not overtake us" (Micah 2:6). Micah, however, rages against such moral and spiritual blindness and presumption. Sarcastically he tells them that the sort of preacher they want is someone who will tell them about the evils of drinking liquor. That's always a good, safe topic for a preacher. After all, who can argue with sermons about the benefits of sobriety? His listeners are probably the most sober people around. Of course they'll listen to sermons on the evils of drunkenness. Such sermons are aimed at somebody else, and those are the sermons that all of us want to hear.

It's easy to be morally outraged at the drug traffic in our inner cities, at the corruption and degradation of the welfare system, at the city schools that are more often battlegrounds than they are places of education, at the racial violence that erupts spectacularly in places like Los Angeles. It's easy to point fingers and assign blame to a particular ethnic group or political party, a particular civic leader or government program. What we don't want to hear is that we ourselves are responsible. That is not something we want to deal with. We don't personally wish to be oppressive or exploitative, we don't personally engage in greedy or overly self-indulgent lifestyles, and so we don't want to hear that we are all, in some way, responsible, or that we are likely to experience the judgment that is inherent in the injustices of our society. Even if we are willing to hear about our own complicity in the oppressive structures of our social order, we often feel helpless to do anything about it. What can one person, or even one congregation, do about such massive, structural and systematic problems?

Our gospel lesson, which is the story of Jesus and the healing of ten people with leprosy, may give us some clues. At first, when I read the lessons for this week, I was stumped. What on earth did this story in Luke's gospel have to do with Micah's harsh indictment of the good, solid, middle-class citizens of ancient Jerusalem? But the more I reflected on them, the more I began to see some connections — not only connections between the two passages of scripture, but connections to my own life and to our life together as the Body of Christ.

The first clue that may hint at some connections is the simple fact that Jesus, in stark contrast to all the social taboos of his day, stopped to listen to the request of a group of lepers. Today, we know that leprosy is not only easily curable with the right medication, but is not very contagious at all. In fact, if one person were married to another who had an active case of Hansen's disease, which is the medical name for leprosy, there would only be a five percent chance of contagious infection. But because leprosy is such a disfiguring disease, it was greatly feared, and in the ancient world, and even today, it is accompanied by strong social taboos. In Jesus' day, to even come into close proximity to a leper was to risk spiritual pollution. And to touch a leper was to incur such pollution that exaggerated rituals of cleansing would be necessary before one was allowed back into polite company. Even the strong enmity between Jews and Samaritans was overcome by the stronger social taboo of leprosy. Nine of the ten lepers were Jews; one was a Samaritan. Their common affliction brought them into community with each other — a community of the socially damned.

It's not difficult to see parallels between the social taboos against leprosy in Jesus' day, and the social taboos against victims of AIDS in our own, is it? *Moody Monthly,* a Christian magazine, reported the story of a woman who called a church and asked the pastor if he would please pray for her son. "Of course, I will," replied the pastor. "Is there something in particular I should pray for?" The mother replied, "He has AIDS. And this is the fifth church I've called to find someone willing to pray for my son. The first two ministers I talked to hung up on me when I told them my son's problem. One simply said no, and one didn't call back when I left a message on the answering machine."

Jesus stopped to listen to a group of people who were the silenced people of his day. The social outcasts. The pariahs. Others went out of their way to avoid any contact with lepers. Jesus stopped, listened, and responded to their request for healing. He went against the grain of his own society's rules and taboos. He risked social ostracism himself in order to minister to those silenced ones, those who were excluded from polite company.

A second clue is in the response of those healed. Ten lepers were healed; nine of them followed Jesus' instructions to go show themselves to the priests in the temple at Jerusalem. To the priests was committed the responsibility for admitting or excluding someone from the community. Since leprosy excluded a person from the community, a priest had to pronounce that a person was cured of leprosy in order for him to be readmitted into society. So the nine lepers did what Jesus told them, went to the priests, and presumably were readmitted into society and became solid middle-class citizens once again. And although Luke doesn't say so directly, it might not be stretching the point too far to think that once readmitted, they might have conformed to society's values and taboos themselves. They probably took up despising Samaritans again just like the rest of polite society.

But one leper came back to Jesus to thank him and to give praise to God for his healing. And to top it off, he was the doubly damned one — the Samaritan. Jesus expressed astonishment that the only one who had enough gratitude to praise God for his healing was this despised foreigner, this one who was double the outsider, both because of his leprosy and because he was a Samaritan. And Jesus' statement to this grateful man hits us like a stroke of lightning. "Go your way, your faith has saved you." Jesus had already healed him of leprosy. But now, he receives something more as a result of his gratitude to God for the blessing of the recovery of his health and readmission to human society: salvation — the wholeness of life, the total well-being that comes to those who depend entirely upon God and not on themselves. That's the word that is used in Jesus' statement — the word salvation. Jesus equates this man's gratitude with faith, faith in God, dependence upon God, trust in God's mercy, and that is the attitude which brings him the blessing of salvation.

The final clue to the connections between this story and Micah's prophecy, and the clue to the connections to our own lives comes in Jesus' answer to the question raised by the Pharisees immediately following this story. It's no accident that Luke places this question and answer right after the story of the salvation of the grateful leper. The Pharisees are the morally upright, deeply religious, and socially respectable citizens of their day. Solid people. Good people. They ask Jesus, "When is the kingdom of God coming?" Jesus replies, "The kingdom of God is not coming with spectacular signs; in fact, the kingdom of God is among you." What does this mean? It means that the kingdom of God is present where we are least disposed to look, especially if we're the solid, respectable, morally upright, hard-working, salt-of-the-earth types that we are. It means that we probably ought not to be blinded like the people of Micah's day and think that our prosperity and our solid middle-class values and the fact that we're sober and not drunken sots are the signs of God's kingdom. Rather, the signs of God's kingdom are when people like us, out of gratitude, begin to pay attention to the outcasts, to the silenced, to the socially unacceptable. When we overcome our fears and taboos to minister to AIDS victims, when we offer our time and energies to providing for the needs of children damaged because their parents were drug addicts, when we open our doors to the poor and welcome them among us, when we work for better housing and better health care, even though it may mean paying higher taxes to make it possible, and when we do it because we are grateful that we ourselves have been healed and touched by God, then we know that the kingdom of God is among us.

I know of an urban congregation, an old "downtown" church, which took some bold steps in 1987 to reach out to the silenced and excluded people of the inner city. Most of them were not residents of the inner city themselves. For the most part, they were respectable, middle-class people who lived in the suburbs. But their church had been standing on the central square of the city for many years. Through all the prosperity of the '50s, the social revolution of the '60s and the urban blight of the '70s, they had stayed downtown because they knew they had a mission there, even if it wasn't always clear to them what it was or how to go about it.

But it was becoming obvious that they needed help to fulfill it. And so, in cooperation with a sister church in the affluent suburbs, they began an Urban Mission Project amid many uncertainties, with inadequate planning, inadequate funds, and little idea where it would all lead, if anywhere. And God honored that vision. They hired a full-time staff person skilled in urban ministry to coordinate their efforts. The program, however, was dependent upon the participation of many volunteers from the two congregations.

With financial strain an ever-present companion, they began ministries with inner city children, homeless men, and welfare mothers — ministries which have brought hope and transformed lives to many who were without hope. Before that bold step, people in the city used to ask if there was still an active congregation at that church; it always looked as though it were closed. Now, no one asks that question. Now that church is known as the church which is "doing something" in the city, and other churches and city officials alike look to that congregation for a model of what ordinary people who care can do.

When asked why they took such a risk of faith to reach out to people at the bottom of the social and economic ladder, many of those who volunteer in the various ministries simply reply that they feel it's the least they can do in light of all of God's blessings which they enjoy. In other words, they are grateful. Gratitude motivates them and enables them to be beacons of hope to those without hope.

D. T. Niles, the Indian theologian, once defined evangelism as "one hungry beggar telling another hungry beggar where to find bread." When we are grateful enough for the bread that we have received that we are willing to reach out to the lost and hurting and lonely and excluded ones around us, we will discover that we ourselves are being saved.

Proper 24
Pentecost 22
Ordinary Time 29
Luke 18:1-8 (C, RC)
Luke 18:1-8a (L)

Tough Faith
In Tough Times

Two qualities which we Americans value highly and in which we take pride are speed and efficiency. Think of how many products or services which all of us use that are built principally around one or both of these qualities. Hundreds of thousands of microwave ovens have been sold, not because they make food taste better, but because it's possible to cook much faster in them. Since so many people lead such busy lives, anything that shortens time in the kitchen has an instant appeal.

A colleague told of meeting a woman from West Germany at a seminar on prayer in Princeton. She was marvelling over one of our speedy and efficient inventions, the tea bag. She said that the Germans don't make teabags, and she found it a very convenient way to have a cup of tea. Of course, she then went on to mention that teabags didn't produce nearly as tasty a cup of tea as loose tea does.

Our banking procedures are also marvels of efficiency. A friend who served as a missionary in Malaysia always used to complain that it took him anywhere from 20-45 minutes to cash his paycheck because of the inefficient banking procedures. Instead of having each teller be a cashier as we do, the tellers and the cashiers were different people. The teller looked over your check, made sure that your deposit slip was filled out correctly, got the initials of one of the bank officers on the cashier's approval slip, and then placed it on the bottom of the pile of similar checks waiting to be cashed by the cashier who sat enclosed in a little cubicle. After standing in line at the teller's counter, one then went over and stood in line at the cashier's counter, and waited some more. Cashing a paycheck was a great lesson in patience each month, a quality that we Americans are notably short on.

Because of our cultural preference for speed and efficiency, our gospel lesson this morning has something to say to us that each of us needs very much to hear. The themes of patient waiting, of persistence, of faithfulness in the face of the seeming indifference of God to our troubles are addressed by this rather strange story in Luke's gospel.

The story of the "unjust judge" as it's often called, raises an age-old human question: why, if God is righteous, is he so slow in seeing that justice is done? Why does it seem like justice is constantly perverted? Why doesn't God act quickly and efficiently to rectify injustice and vindicate those who are righteous and punish those who are wicked? It's probably the most common human complaint and question there is, isn't it? Is there any one of us who hasn't asked it scores of times?

When we read in *Newsweek* about the terrible situation in Bosnia, we ask, "Why doesn't God intervene in some way?" When we hear of the massacres of innocent people including children in Rwanda and Burundi, we shiver at the horror of it all and wonder why the people of those lands cannot see that ancient rivalries are preventing them from achieving prosperity in the modern world.

Closer to home, we see the blight in our inner cities; we deplore the violence that is so frequently related to the drug traffic in areas of poverty. Since our orientation is toward problem-solving, we look for immediate solutions. Get tough on drug dealers. Mandatory prison sentences, more police, cut off aid to Colombia. Yet our solutions don't seem to solve the problem. They have the virtue of speed and efficiency, but the problems themselves prove more recalcitrant and intractable than we imagined. Because we lack patience and the persistence to search for solutions that may not be speedy and efficient, but which, in the long term, would be more effective, we become frustrated and lose interest. Long-term issues don't have much media appeal.

The same holds true for our personal lives as for our social and international problems. Our washing machine breaks down, and we immediately call the repairman. Problem solved. But let us break a hip or develop a heart condition, and we lose patience quickly. We get depressed or we become complainers. We want to be back at full steam, and we don't like having to wait.

Jesus' parable of the persistent widow and the unjust judge offers a corrective to our impatience and our fascination with short-term problem-solving. The experience of the widow is one which is instantly familiar to us. We've all known the frustrations of delay in having our needs and wants gratified. We've all known what it's like to be treated unjustly; we've all known what it's like to have our plea for fairness, for justice, go unheard or unheeded. Those who have ever tried to reason with an IRS auditor know exactly how this poor widow felt. The cards were stacked against her. The judge may even have been in league with her opponent who was exploiting her in some way. The widow cries to the judge for justice, and the only reason she eventually gets it is because the judge gets weary of listening to her lament. She wears him down with her persistence until he finally does the right thing just to get rid of her.

Interpreters of this parable have sometimes made the mistake of turning this parable into an allegory, assigning the role of the judge to God. Not only does that cause us to miss the main point, it also casts God in a very unflattering light. The parable does urge us to be like the widow, praying persistently without giving up. But the only point of contact between God and the judge is one of contrast. God is *not* like the unjust judge, and God's response to our persistent requests will not be like the response of the unjust judge to the widow's pleas. In contrast to the judge who delays because of his venality or his indifference, God "will quickly grant justice to his chosen ones who cry out to him." Jesus says. He won't delay long in helping them like the unjust judge delayed helping the woman. God's help will come speedily. The emphasis is not on the negative picture of justice which the parable itself portrays, but rather on the contrast between the reluctance of the unjust judge and the willingness of God to act on behalf of those who cry out to him. If a corrupt and unjust judge will render justice because the plaintiff is so persistent, how much more is God, who loves us and is concerned about us, willing to answer us when we call to him?

In view of the parable's insistence that God will bring justice and bring it speedily, what then are we to make of our sense that God seems to be taking his own sweet time about fulfilling his promises to make things right? The parable suggests a two-fold answer: In the first place, our notion of when and how a problem ought to be solved does not necessarily correspond to God's solutions. That's why the widow can represent the human side of the experience of waiting for justice, but the judge does not represent God's response. God, however, does not operate by human time-clocks. God sees the end from the beginning, and he answers the cry of his people speedily, but speedily in relation to God's own knowledge of the situation and according to his own timetable. It is our impatience and our desire to have every problem solved immediately that leads us to experience the situation as justice delayed.

I heard a story which illustrates how we often confuse God's timing with ours. A country newspaper had been running a series of articles on the value of church attendance. One day, a letter to the editor was received in the newspaper office. It read, "Print this if you dare. I have been trying an experiment. I have a field of corn which I plowed on Sunday. I planted it on Sunday. I did all the cultivating on Sunday. I gathered the harvest on Sunday and hauled it to my barn on Sunday.

I find that my harvest this October is just as great as any of my neighbors' who went to church on Sunday. So where was God all this time?" The editor printed the letter, but added his reply at the bottom. "Your mistake was in thinking that God always settles his accounts in October." That's often our mistake as well, isn't it — thinking that God should act when and how we want him to act, according to our timetable rather than his. The fact that our vision is limited, finite, unable to see the end from the beginning, somehow escapes our mind. So we complain; we get frustrated; we accuse God of being indifferent to us; we do not live by faith.

In fact, it may be our actions or behavior that cause what we experience as delay or unfair treatment. God always takes human freedom seriously. God does not will the ancient feuds in Rwanda and Burundi, nor does he will the violence that they spawn. But he does will human beings to be free to make decisions, even if those decisions are motivated by evil or wrong desires. So while God is at work to bring about his ends, he is at work through human individuals and human agencies, despite the injustice that often characterizes human relationships, because God respects our freedom.

In the second place, it is not our part, while waiting in patience to complain or to sulk or to be passive, but to be faithful and persistent in prayer. This is why Jesus says that we ought always to pray and not to lose heart. It is not our part to set the terms of how justice will be meted out; our part is to be faithful in prayer and faithful in life, and our faithfulness will enable us to wait in patience for God to act, even though in our limited time frame, we may not see God's will accomplished like we would like to see it.

Such persistence in prayer is what faithfulness to God is all about. It means refusing to give in to appearances and continuing to trust God to act in his way and in his time. It may appear that God does not hear. It may appear that we are alone and without supernatural help. It may appear that injustice and evil are prevailing. But faith dares to go on praying, to grasp the reality that we cannot see and live by it. This is really what makes people of faith different from others. We are willing to live by what we cannot see, but which we believe to be real, rather than by what we can see, and which the world, or our culture, tells us is real. Only someone who believes in a reality that is unseen will persist in praying. Everybody prays, but many people only pray when they're in a jam and are desperate because they can't come up with any fast and efficient human solution.

If we do not experience the power of God in our lives, it is probably due more to our failure to pray persistently than it is to God's reluctance to answer. When we don't get the answer we expect when we expect it, the temptation is to stop praying and start asking why. That is not faith; it is not faithful living. And the end of our gospel lesson drives this point home. For after affirming God's willingness to hear our prayers and vindicate his people, Jesus poses this very poignant question, "Nevertheless, when the Son of Man comes, will he find faith on earth?" The real question is not about God's faithfulness, but about ours. The message of Luke is that God is faithful; therefore, the way to experience God's faithfulness is for us to have faith in him, to live by faith in God, to persist in trusting God, even when appearances do not seem to support either his existence or his concern for us. The righteous person lives by faith.

"When the Son of Man comes, will he find faith on the earth?" That is the question this parable asks of each of us. Where is the point in your life at which you need to let go of your fears, your frustrations, your impatience, your anger, and sink down into patient trust in God's timing and in his way of working? There's a point like that in each of our lives, a point where we need to let go of our desire for speed and efficiency and just sit back and let God work in his way and in his time, all the while living faithfully and praying persistently.

Proper 25
Pentecost 23
Ordinary Time 30
Luke 18:9-14

The Good, The Bad, And The Justified

The famous actor Gregory Peck was once standing in line with a friend, waiting for a table in a crowded Los Angeles restaurant. They had been waiting for some time, the diners seemed to be taking their time eating and new tables weren't opening up very fast. They weren't even that close to the front of the line. Peck's friend became impatient, and he said to Gregory Peck, "Why don't you tell the maitre d' who you are?" Gregory Peck responded with great wisdom. "No," he said, "if you have to tell them who you are, then you aren't."

That's a lesson that the Pharisee in our gospel reading apparently had never learned. His prayer, if it can be called that, is largely an advertisement for himself. He's selling himself to God. Little wonder that Luke describes him in the way he does, "The Pharisee stood and prayed thus with himself." That's a very apt description, isn't it — he prayed *with himself.* He would have done better had he had Gregory Peck there to whisper in his ear that if he had to remind God who he was, then he wasn't.

The tax collector, on the other hand, didn't have to tell God who he was. He knew who he was and he knew that God knew who he was. His prayer is not an exercise in self-promotion, but a confession and a plea for mercy. He is not selling himself, but opening himself. And Jesus says, "It is this man who went home justified." To be justified means to be declared "not guilty." It means to be declared right. The tax collector is declared to be in the right relationship to God while the Pharisee, who is so certain of his own righteousness, is shown to be in the wrong relationship with God. He is not justified before the bar of God's justice which is the court of ultimate consequence.

We hasten to add, however, that this does not mean that the Pharisee was a bad person and the tax collector really a good person. There's no suggestion of that in this parable. The Pharisee was probably every bit as good and moral and generous as he claimed to be. When he gives that little speech about how he fasts and tithes and gives alms and prays frequently, he's not guilty of false advertising. There's no suggestion that he's a hypocrite — pretending to be something he isn't. In fact, the Pharisees enjoyed great respect among the people of Israel because of the high standards of their morality, their ethics, and their piety. Nor is there any suggestion that the tax collector was really a good guy at heart — something akin to the Hollywood version of the prostitute with the heart of gold or the thief who robs only from the rich in order to give to the poor. The tax collector was very likely every bit as bad as his reputation made him out to be. If he hadn't been crooked, he wouldn't have been a tax collector in the first place, for the Romans couldn't get honest people to be their lackeys. The only people who would serve as tax collectors were people who were interested in enriching themselves with little concern for how they did it. The contrast in the parable is not between the real, but hidden, goodness of the tax collector and the real, but hidden, hypocrisy of the Pharisee. Such a construction misses the point. If that were the case, it would not be at all hard to understand why it is the tax collector and not the Pharisee who is declared to be righteous and who goes home justified.

No, this parable is much more radical than that, and it is so because the gospel is radical. It goes to the root of the problem of human sinfulness and alienation from God. The gospel that Jesus proclaims in this parable is radical in at least three aspects: first, the parable tells us that God knows us as we really are; second, that God accepts us as we are; and third, that though God accepts us as we are, he never leaves us as we are.

The first of those three aspects of the gospel is familiar to us, though we may not live in awareness of it all the time. *God knows who we are.* We don't have to do a snow-job on God and sell ourselves to him. Like the line in the Christmas song about Santa Claus, "he knows if you've been bad or good," God knows us. But God's knowledge of us goes much deeper than that. He knows not only our actions, but our motives, our intentions, our deepest and most intimate secrets, he even knows what is in the depths of our unconscious minds. The psalmist said it well when he said, "While I was in my mother's womb, while I was being created in secret, behold, O Lord, you knew me altogether" (Psalm 139:13, 15).

Such knowledge can be a frightening thing if we operate on the "God rewards the good and punishes the bad" philosophy. If that is the way things work, then I'm in trouble, because I've got things inside me that I wouldn't want anyone else to know. There are parts of me that are too private, too painful, too intimate to share with anyone. So if I think that my acceptance by God depends on him not knowing about who I really am inside, then I'm lost. That's why the news that God knows exactly who I am, better than I know myself, is such a liberating piece of good news. I don't have to pretend. I am who God knows me to be. I don't have to be afraid of him finding out something I'm ashamed of, I don't have to close off part of my life to him; he knows me with a knowledge that is deep and wonderful and intimate and infinite. Paul reminds us that when our time comes to finally stand in God's presence our own knowledge will be full and complete: "One day," he says, "I shall know, even as I am fully known" (1 Corinthians 13:12). What a wonderful prospect! So if you've got something to hide, don't bother. God already knows more about you than you will ever know until that day when he grants you fullness of knowledge and that will be heaven.

But close on the heels of this truth, comes the next part. *God not only knows who I am, but he accepts me as I am.* I say this is radical because it goes right against the grain of the way most of us think. If something good happens to somebody we know, we say, "Well, you must be living right," meaning that their goodness has been rewarded. When something bad happens to us, we immediately begin to wonder what we've done to cause God to punish us. It is normal for us to think that God blesses those who are good and punishes those who are bad. That's the way we would do it if we were God, and we project our own ideas of justice and reward and punishment onto God. The only problem with that is that God doesn't quite fit our expectations of him. As Karl Barth, the great theologian, would say, "God is God." He is not an idol created in our image. God is God. God acts as *God* acts. And Jesus says in this parable that God is a God who justifies the ungodly. He declares sinners to be in right relation to himself. He declares them not guilty. By human standards of justice, this is positively scandalous. God justifies the ungodly? Why? Because they are ungodly? No! God hates their ungodliness. Then why does he justify them? Because they trust in him for their justification, and that is the right or righteous thing to do. To throw oneself on the mercy of God is the right thing to do and God declares us righteous when we do it. That is the meaning of having faith or believing — having faith in God, believing that God will act like God and have mercy on us. The problem most of us have is that we don't act like God, and therefore, we are scandalized when God acts like God.

Samuel Colgate, the founder of the Colgate business empire, was a devout Christian, and he told of an incident that took place in the church he attended. During an evangelistic service, an invitation was given at the close of the sermon for all those who wished to turn their lives over to Christ and be forgiven. One of the first persons to walk down the aisle and kneel at the altar was a well-known prostitute. She knelt in very real repentance, she wept, she asked God to forgive her, and meanwhile the rest of the congregation looked on approvingly at what she was doing. Then she stood and testified that she believed God had forgiven her for her past life, and she now wanted to become a member of the church. For a few moments, the silence was deafening. Finally, Samuel Colgate arose and said, "I guess we blundered when we prayed that the Lord would save sinners. We forgot to specify what kind of sinners. We'd better ask him to forgive us for this oversight. The Holy Spirit has touched this woman and made her truly repentant, but the Lord apparently doesn't understand that she's not the type we want him to rescue. We'd better spell it out for him just which sinners we had in mind." Immediately, a motion was made and unanimously approved that the woman be accepted into membership in the congregation.

God accepts us as we are. There's not a sin too black, not a deed too awful, not a thought too horrible for him to forgive. What cuts us off from his forgiveness and the freedom such forgiveness brings is our thinking that we have to justify ourselves. Trusting in our own righteousness does not bring God's verdict of not guilty. Trusting in God's righteousness does.

But if we say that God justifies the ungodly, doesn't that appear to condone bad or sinful behavior? If God doesn't require us to change before he accepts us, then what's the use of being good at all? Why not sin boldly and have a good time? After all, the scriptures say that there is pleasure in sin, for a time. Ah, but here the third truth comes into play. God knows who we are; he accepts us as we are; *but he never leaves us as we are.* When God justifies us on the basis of our faith in him, he also transforms us and makes us better than we are.

The theological or biblical term for God's forgiving and claiming work in us is justification. The word for God's cleansing and purifying within us is sanctification. God starts with us just where he find us, whether in the palace or the pig sty, but he never leaves us there. For God's purpose is not just to rescue us from hell but to get us ready for heaven. So he's in the business of making us holy, or to put it as the writer of Ephesians 4:15 does, helping us "to grow up in every way into Christ who is our head." Maturity in Christ, spiritual adulthood, perfection in love — these are all ways to describe God's work in our lives subsequent to the moment when he justifies us, or declares us righteous.

This sanctifying work of God's spirit within us, does not turn us into stained-glass saints, people who walk around piously with their hands folded in prayer all day. God's work within us is the most practical, down-to-earth (or perhaps we should say up-to-heaven) work imaginable. When we open our lives to his gracious presence, when we no longer trust in our own morality or good behavior or willpower, we find the most amazing things beginning to happen. As we experience more of God's love for us, we find ourselves becoming more loving toward others. People with bad tempers find that God's spirit within them enables them to control their temper. People with enslaving habits like alcoholism or addiction to gambling, find a resource that is beyond themselves and a source of strength to overcome those diseases of the soul. People with too much love of money and material things find that their values begin to change. People with deep insecurities and low self-esteem begin to see themselves and love themselves as God loves them and sees them.

This doesn't all happen at once, of course. Discipleship, sanctification, spiritual maturity, whatever you want to call it, is a life-long process. It's a journey. We don't become saints overnight, but we do *become*. That's the nature of the Christian life — becoming conformed to the image of Christ.

The transforming work of the Holy Spirit in the life of a believer was the chief theme of John Wesley's life and work, and a distinctive contribution the Methodists make to the rest of the church. Wesley had a four-fold dictum: "All people need to be saved from sin; all people can be saved from sin; all people can know they are saved from sin; and all people can be saved to the uttermost." It is that latter that Wesley particularly emphasized. He called it "going on to perfection." He didn't mean a sinless kind of moral perfection, not a perfection in knowledge, but a perfection in love. The single identifying mark of the Holy Spirit's work in our lives is love. Do we love God and do we love one another? That's the test of our sanctification.

Wesley was always deeply disturbed when he saw Christians who were more like the Pharisee than the tax collector — people who trusted in their own righteousness, and consequently, showed little evidence of the growing presence of God's love in their lives. Once while he was preaching, he noticed a lady in the congregation who was known for her critical attitudes toward others. All through the service she stared at his tie, with a frown on her face. At the end of the service, she came up to him and said very sharply, "Mr. Wesley, the strings on your bow tie are much too long. It offends me." Wesley immediately asked for a pair of scissors, and when someone handed them to him, he gave them to the woman and said, "Then by all means, trim it to your satisfaction." She did so, clipping off an inch or so from each side. "Are you sure they're all right now," he asked, and she replied, "Yes, that's much better."

"Then let me have the scissors for a moment," Wesley said, "for I'm sure you won't mind a bit of correction either. I do not wish to be cruel, madam, but your tongue offends me — it is too long. Please stick it out so that I may trim some of it off." Needless to say, this critic got the point.

Now God may not take a pair of scissors to our tongue, but for some of us, that may be the part of us where he chooses to begin his sanctifying work, for it is one of the things by which we give most offense and sin against love. But whether it's our tongue or our ambition or our lust or our prejudice or our materialism or our pride or our self-righteousness, or whatever else our besetting sin may be, God will not be content until Christ's image is perfectly formed in us, and that is why he will never leave us as he finds us. Like a dentist who will insist on pulling the tooth with the abscess in it, rather than merely giving us some pain-killer, God will insist on removing the abscesses from our souls. We do not have to remove them to make ourselves acceptable to him; he accepts us warts and all, as the saying goes. But he will insist on giving us the full treatment, causing us a lesser pain in order to spare us an infinitely greater one — the pain of a life without him.

What aspect of the gospel speaks most to your needs? Is it the fact that God knows you, and knows you intimately and fully? If so, then accept the freedom that God offers you. Open yourself to him, confess who you are to him, and you will find him gracious. Perhaps it is the second aspect which speaks most keenly to you — that God accepts you as you are and declares us righteous on the basis of your trust in him. That too is liberating. Not only do you not have to hide your real self, but you do not have to make yourself good. Accept his love. Accept his forgiveness which he offers you in Christ. Accept his claim upon you. Accept your adoption into the family of God. Or maybe you've experienced that much of the gospel — the knowledge that you are loved and accepted and justified — but you have not experienced the transforming work of the Spirit in your life, because you have not understood or because you have not been open to allow him to work. If so, then open yourself to the Spirit as fully as you are consciously capable of doing; give him the freedom to cleanse away all that is incompatible with the love of Christ, accept his discipline, commit yourself to "going in for the full treatment." This, too, is a work of faith, a matter of trust, for we do not make ourselves holy. It is God who makes us like Christ. We will not have better morals or better ethics or more willpower when we decide to. We will have them when we allow God to change our inner nature into conformity with the nature of Christ. When Christ is formed in us, then we will be better people with better behavior. So our salvation from God's knowledge of us in our mother's wombs to our perfected knowledge of ourselves and of him in heaven is the work of his grace and the product of faith. From beginning to end, we are saved by God's grace.

Proper 26
Pentecost 24
Ordinary Time 31
Luke 19:1-10

Out On A Limb

A friend told me of the hours he spent as a child in a large cherry tree in his grandmother's backyard. The tree was very large and high, at least as he remembered it. He remembered the very first time he climbed it. He had to jump to catch hold of the lowest branch, and then pull himself by sheer muscle power up onto it. Then he could work his way up the tree. The tree seemed so high, that he got dizzy looking down, and yet, scary as it was, he couldn't resist climbing higher and higher. Finally he got very close to the top where the branches were thinner, and he could climb no higher. He stayed there, straddling a limb and holding tightly to one above it, swaying in the breeze with the leaves fluttering around him. It was an exhilarating moment for a seven-year-old. He was on top of the world.

But when the time came to climb back down, he was terrified. As long as he was on his way up, his vision and his focus was on the branch above him. But on the way down, all he could see was how far below the ground was and how many protruding limbs there were between him and the ground. Very gingerly, he made his way down, branch by branch, and when he finally got on the ground, he discovered his knees were trembling with the excitement and fear of the whole experience. Like a typical small boy, however, once he knew he could conquer the tree, he couldn't stay out of it, and before long, he went up and down it like a monkey. Somehow, the risk of being out on a limb high in the tree became as routine as brushing one's teeth.

Years later, long after he had grown out of his tree-climbing days, he was visiting his grandparents and happened to notice the old cherry tree. The lower limb that had been his first step up into the tree, the limb that he had had to leap to catch hold of, now was at shoulder height. The whole tree seemed somehow shrunken and unprepossessing. It wasn't nearly as large as he remembered it. The thin branches near the top, where he had spent many a summer hour swaying in the breezes and feeling himself to be on top of the world, were no more than 20 feet from the ground. He laughed as he saw the tree through the adult eyes, but he remembered and relived for a few moments, his feelings as that seven-year-old boy with trembling knees taking a daring risk to climb up among the clouds.

The gospel lesson for today is about another tree-climber whose name was Zacchaeus. He too experienced the risk and exhilaration of being "out on a limb." Zacchaeus' life was transformed as he sat on his tree limb, and at the time, it must have been a thoroughly scary experience, though perhaps later, as a mature disciple, he may have wondered why it ever seemed risky or frightening at all.

Luke, alone, tells us this story. He places it in the context of his account of Jesus' journey to Jerusalem. Following Mark's gospel, one of his main sources, he relates the story of Jesus' healing of a blind man near the city of Jericho. But then he adds this story about Jesus' encounter with a man named Zacchaeus.

Jesus is just passing through Jericho, Luke tells us. He apparently didn't have any pressing engagements there. He wasn't contemplating a preaching mission or healings. He was just passing through. He was going to Jerusalem. Jerusalem was the focus of his vision at this point. He had a rendezvous with destiny, and nothing would deter him from keeping it. So Jericho is just a way station, a place one had to go through to get to Jerusalem. Yet, it becomes the place of a significant encounter.

This is often the case, isn't it? The places and situations that we consider temporary or simply way stations turn out to be the places or situations that hold the most significance for us. Henri Nouwen once said something to the effect that in his ministry he found himself becoming frustrated and resentful that his work was constantly being interrupted by people who wanted or needed something from him, until one day the Lord spoke to him and revealed that his real work was in those interruptions. So I think we have to pay attention to the transit points on our journey. It just may be that we'll discover someone, perhaps even ourselves, who is out on a limb and needs some attention.

If Jericho did not figure prominently in Jesus' plans, however, Jesus' transit through Jericho certainly loomed large in Zacchaeus' mind, as well as in the mind of other citizens of the town. We're only told two facts about Zacchaeus: he was the chief tax collector, and he was short. Whether there was any relationship between those two facts, we don't know. Luke has not delved into Zacchaeus' psychological makeup, so we don't have any basis for addressing that question. But those two facts do figure prominently in the story.

As chief tax collector, Zacchaeus was a traitor to his people and nation. He was a collaborator and agent of the imperialist Romans who had imposed their rule on Palestine by military conquest and occupation. At a time when zealot movements were springing up to oppose Roman rule through guerilla warfare, tax collectors were the pariahs of society. Zacchaeus may have seen himself as a practitioner of "realpolitik," but his countrymen saw him as a thief and a traitor. I say thief, because though Rome required a certain amount in taxes from its colonial subjects, it also turned a blind eye to how much the tax collector was able to gouge for his own pockets above and beyond the required sum. So long as he was not so greedy that he incited actual revolt, he was free to fleece his fellow-citizens for as much as he could get them to cough up. So Zacchaeus was not exactly the most popular fellow in Jericho, though undoubtedly he was one of the best-known. And certainly, he would never need fear that people were indifferent to him.

The other fact also is important — that he was short. For it is this fact that moves the action in the story. His shortness of stature prevents him from seeing over the people lining the street to catch a glimpse of Jesus and his company as they pass through Jericho. Everybody loves a parade, and no excuse is too trivial. So the townspeople are out to see this man whose reputation has preceded him from Galilee where he has spent most of his life and ministry. They're not about to make way for this shrimp of a tax collector.

So Zacchaeus is forced to do something he probably hasn't done since he was a boy. He climbs a tree. Apparently he hasn't lost his tree-climbing skills from when he was a small boy. Actually, climbing a tree is like riding a bike; once you learn you never really forget how to do it. Your joints may be less flexible and more creaky, but you still know how to do it. So Zacchaeus gets up into the tree, and eases his way out onto a limb so he will have a good view of Jesus when he passes by. (I can imagine the remarks that others are making when they see this, and the crude attempts at humor that compare Zacchaeus to his ancestors the apes.)

When Jesus comes along, he stops beneath the tree and says, "Zacchaeus, hurry and come down; for I must stay at your house today." And Luke says, "So he hurried down and was happy to welcome him." Wait a minute. Hasn't Luke left out a lot here? He hasn't told us how Jesus knew Zacchaeus' name, nor even intimated that Zacchaeus must have nearly fallen out of his tree when he heard himself being addressed by this Galilean rabbi he's heard about, but never laid eyes on before. We're left to wonder about the details. Did Zacchaeus flatter himself by thinking that his own reputation had spread to Galilee, so that his name was a household word? Was he stricken with a sense of awe and dread that a total stranger should come right to where he was hanging out on a limb and stop and call him by name? Had somebody ratted on him to Jesus to cause trouble for him? We don't know. All this is left to our imaginations. The story itself is laconic and spare. Jesus calls; Zacchaeus responds. Just like that.

We're not left to imagine the reaction of the other people standing around, however. They are clearly unhappy. Here they are, all good, law-abiding, patriotic citizens who know whom to despise and whom to approve. Jesus' attentions to Zacchaeus are not appreciated at all by the other onlookers. Why should he single out Zacchaeus to provide the honor of hospitality rather than some of them who remain steadfast in their hatred of the Romans and in their support of nationalistic aspirations? Why go stay in the home of a sinner? It's one thing to love sinners in the abstract; it's another to sleep in their houses. In the Middle East, even today, providing hospitality to others is considered a great honor and solemn duty. It's hard for us to grasp the real import of what is happening here. For us, playing the host is sometimes seen as a duty that has to be performed, but we're always glad when our guests go away and we get the house back to ourselves. But Jesus, by inviting Zacchaeus to provide him with hospitality is paying Zacchaeus honor and respect. He is, quite literally, gracing Zacchaeus with his presence.

But if Zacchaeus was "out on a limb" in the literal sense, he's even more "out on a limb" when he stands before Jesus. Jesus' invitation to come down out of his tree, and his unexpected and gracious offer to come stay in his house calls forth from Zacchaeus a similarly unexpected and grace-filled response. It's a response that is far more risky and scary than his climb up into the branches of the tree ever was. "Lord, half of my possessions I will give to the poor, and if I have defrauded anyone of anything, I will pay back four times as much." Now that's what I call conversion!

Jesus has not demanded anything of Zacchaeus. Rather he has offered him the opportunity to play the magnanimous host, giving Zacchaeus stature far beyond his natural height.

Yet this offer of grace, for that's what it is, calls forth a willingness on Zacchaeus' part to respond in kind. Jesus hasn't censured him for being a tax collector. He hasn't said a word about his sinful gouging of his fellow citizens to enrich his own coffers. He hasn't breathed the word "traitor." He's just announced his intention to stay with Zacchaeus. And yet that offer presents Zacchaeus with a demand that is far more fraught with risk than anything he has ever done or dreamed of doing. Or perhaps, he has dreamed of doing it. Perhaps that's where this blurted out promise of generosity comes from — from Zacchaeus' dreams of being a better person than he is. As he stands before Jesus, perhaps he sees himself, not as he is, a morally-stunted and hated tax collector, but as the benefactor of the poor and the righter of wrongs that he may become.

That's really being "out on a limb," isn't it — to see ourselves as we might become, and to commit ourselves to begin living by that vision rather than by what we think of ourselves or what others think of us? It's a scary risk to catch a vision of what we might become with the help of grace. It's risky to let go of our comfort zones, our status quo, our familiar sins, our cherished self-images, and stand before Jesus exposed for what we are, and exposed to what we may become.

I suggest to you that the encounter with the living Christ produces just that effect in us. We see ourselves in a light we never saw ourselves in before. We see that we are as unworthy and sinful as we admit in the privacy of our own hearts, and that we may become better and more useful than we hardly dared to dream. I am not offering a psychologizing version of personal transformation here. This encounter with the living Christ which calls forth from us qualities of character and behavior we never knew or allowed, but perhaps always hoped, we had, is nothing less than a miracle of grace. It is, in fact, what salvation is all about. When Jesus says, "Today salvation has come to this house," he is responding to this "blurted out" new self that Zacchaeus has just discovered — this self that is concerned about justice and restitution. Salvation is becoming who we really are in Christ, and then living that new self out in concrete ways that manifest God's redeeming work in the world.

The crowd of good people who grumbled at grace that day don't seem to have profited by their encounter with Jesus. It is they who hear Jesus' reminder that the Son of Man came to seek and to save the lost. For those who grumble at grace never experience it. Those who risk accepting it discover that their lives are changed forever. So salvation came to Zacchaeus because he was willing to go out on a limb to see Jesus. And salvation comes to us when we are willing to go out on a limb and risk becoming all that we can be through the grace of that same Jesus Christ.

Reformation Sunday
John 8:31-36

The Son Makes Us Free

On a television movie about a family of Virginia plantation owners during the Civil War, one of the sons married a woman whom his family despised because she was not of their class. She was the daughter of a poor "dirt farmer," without the privileged education, carefully cultivated social graces, or the wealth of the family who lived in the big house on the plantation. She became pregnant with their first child shortly before her husband went off to war with Jeb Stuart's calvary, and reluctantly, the family took her into their home on the plantation to care for her and the baby she was carrying. As a wedding gift, they gave her a young slave woman to be her own personal body servant. This made her feel extremely uncomfortable, for she came from people who had never owned slaves and were little higher on the social totem pole than slaves themselves.

In one scene, she had a bad fall, and after arrival home, she had a miscarriage. As she lay in bed, sobbing out her grief at losing the baby, her personal slave was trying to console her. But she refused to be consoled. She said to the slave woman, "You don't know what it's like to lose a child." At that, tears began to trickle down the slave woman's face, and she replied, "Oh yes, I do. They took my baby away from me when he was two years old and sold him to another family, and I've never seen him since."

At that, the two women discovered a bond between them. They knew then that a mother's hurt and pain at losing a child knows no social or racial boundaries. And from that point on, they began to relate to one another as equals. For both of them, there was a kind of liberation, and the young white woman began to understand fully, for the first time, perhaps, the evils of a system that could buy and sell human beings like cattle.

The system of slavery was evil for many reasons, but perhaps the most important was that it was based on a refusal to acknowledge the image of God in other human beings whose differences in skin color, culture, and historical circumstances made it possible for them to be subjugated and reduced to economic commodities. As we've discovered, the captivity of slavery was far greater than the captivity of the body of the slave. Both slaveowner and slave were captives to a system that was corrupt. And this corrupt system which deprived both of their liberty as children of God was itself the product of a deeper, underlying captivity — a captivity to which Jesus, in our gospel lesson, refers as slavery to sin.

Language about sin has nearly disappeared from our modern vocabulary. Only religious people use it, and not even very often or in a particularly well-informed way at that. Our culture prefers to use the language of "psychobabble" to explain the forces that drive human beings, forces that seem to come from deep within or from outside. We talk of someone having a compulsion or an obsession which makes him or her behave in certain ways. Or we speak of someone acting neurotically. And as psychiatry takes an increasingly materialistic turn, we increasingly attribute eccentric or even horrible behavior to chemical imbalance in the brain, treatable, if not completely curable, by various psychotropic drug therapies. Twenty or so years ago, the famous psychiatrist Karl Menninger, with keen insight and foresight, lamented the loss of religious language to explain human behavior in his best-selling book, *Whatever Became of Sin?*

Although religious people occasionally talk about sin, we tend to speak of "sins" rather than "sin." Usually we think of individual acts of wrongdoing or moral lapses. We may say that someone who tells a lie commits a sin, or we may teach our children that stealing is a sin. We may even describe rich desserts as "sinful" or the act of eating a piece of chocolate cheesecake as a "sin," but we usually speak this way just as we're about to attack the piece of cheesecake with great delight. The very fact that we trivialize the word "sin" in this way demonstrates how irrelevant a concept it has become in our personal value system and world view. We do not often speak of sin as a motivating power which drives us to act the way we do. That language seems archaic or even offensive. We're not sinners, or at least not very bad ones. And besides, God has to grade on the curve, since there are so many more people who behave much worse than we do.

Even pastoral work is often defined more in clinical and psychological terms than in religious terms. Pastors now take courses in "pastoral counselling" rather than in the more time-honored art of "spiritual direction." A semester of Clinical Pastoral Education, or CPE as it's known, has become a requirement for seminary graduation or ordination in many churches. Now I don't mean to suggest in any way that a working knowledge of human psychology and counselling skills aren't important for a pastor, and there are many valuable tools and insights to be gained from a course in CPE. But the very nomenclature of the course, and the fact that it's conducted in a hospital in the context of sickness, and the language it uses, betrays its underlying assumptions about the roots and wellsprings of human behavior, and particularly of destructive behavior. We behave badly, not because we are sinners in need of God's grace, but because we're emotionally disturbed or mentally unbalanced. So the modern pastor, rather than being a specialist in the art of helping the people of God progress through the various stages of spiritual growth into "... maturity, to the measure of the full stature of Christ" (Ephesians 4:13), becomes instead a therapist who helps the congregation work through their hang-ups.

Meanwhile, freedom beckons. And some of us are still in slavery. Just what that slavery entails and the road to freedom that beckons us is may be seen in our gospel lesson in the exchange Jesus has with some of his fellow Jews who had believed in him.

Jesus tells these who have been attracted to him, "If you continue in my word, you are truly my disciples; and you will know the truth, and the truth will make you free." This is truly the "way you spell r-e-l-i-e-f!" This is the recipe for liberation. Notice the terms of the equation: continuing in Jesus' word equals being true disciples which equals knowing the truth which equals freedom. It is characteristic of John to set up such multiple equations throughout his gospel. To say one of the terms of the equation is to say them all. Continuing in Jesus' word results in being truly his disciples. Continuing in Jesus' word is also the same as knowing the truth. Continuing in Jesus' word is the route to freedom. Being truly his disciples is the route to freedom. These are not different or separate steps, which if taken one at a time, lead to freedom, but different expressions for the same reality. The reality is the freedom that comes from being in relationship to Jesus. And being a true disciple, knowing the truth, and continuing in his word are all facets of that one reality.

This explains the misunderstanding of his hearers and the further exchange with them. They fail to grasp the fundamental point Jesus is making, that true freedom is relationship with him. For them, the primary relationship is their identity as children of Abraham, that is, as Jews or children of the covenant. They assert proudly their heritage, and insist with equal pride that they have never been anyone's slaves. Yet, in defining their primary relationship as relationship to the covenant with Abraham rather than to Jesus, they have unknowingly described their slavery. For the covenant with Abraham was based on the premise that slavery was only avoidable in a direct relationship with God by faith. Any attempt to ground one's identity in racial or ethnic or cultural or geographical or social or economic or even kinship ties was to end up a slave. A slave to what? To sin, Jesus answers. "Anyone who commits sin is a slave to sin." There is the word "sin" used both as actions and as a power. Committing "sins" is the result of slavery to "Sin" with a capital S.

The primal sin, behind all individual sins as acts of wrongdoing, is the attempt to define ourselves in relationship to someone or something other than God. Whatever it is around which we orientate our very existence becomes god for us. It may be money, it may be family, it may be our racial group or national origin, or it may simply be our godlike self. If I define myself primarily as an American, so that my American-ness is my primary point of reference, then I am a slave to sin. If I define my "whiteness" as my primary point of reference, then I am a slave to sin. If I live, as so many modern Americans do, by the philosophy "I buy, therefore I am," then I am a slave to sin. That relationship becomes the controlling and defining relationship of my life. And if that relationship is not my relationship with God through Jesus Christ, then I am not free. I am under the control of some alien power, and I cannot avoid behaving in ways that demonstrate that power's control over me.

Jesus speaks the liberating word of the gospel when he says, "If the Son makes you free, you shall be free indeed." How does the Son make us free? When we continue in his word. When we are true followers. When we know the truth. But what do these phrases mean? What does it really mean to continue in Jesus' word?

This notion of continuing or abiding in Jesus' word is a large idea in John's gospel. He uses his images like a kaleidoscope. The same images are combined and re-combined in different ways, so that each time he turns the crank we see something different and yet recognize it as the same. So he speaks of continuing in Jesus' word and of Jesus' words abiding in those who hear them. He speaks of abiding in his words and abiding in his love, and we realize that he means the same thing. He speaks of having given his disciples his word and of them keeping his word, and we realize that he is still talking about the same thing. Later in the gospel, we hear Jesus saying, "You are my friends if you do what I command you . . . this is my commandment, that you love one another, as I have loved you" (John 13:34). And we realize that to keep Jesus' commandments is, for John, the same as continuing in his word and having his word abide in the one who continues in it.

The question how do we continue in Jesus' word, or how can we know the truth or how does the truth make us free (which are three ways of asking the same question) can be answered by the answer to another question, "Whom or what do we love?" The way out of slavery is to ground our fundamental identity in our relationship to God through Jesus Christ by continuing in his word, and the way we continue in his word is to love one another as he has loved us.

All this could sound very mystical, but not very well-defined in real life. But perhaps returning to the opening story about the relationship between the white slave-owner and her black slave can help us put flesh and blood on this ethereal-sounding recipe for freedom. The liberation of both the slave and the slave-owner began at the moment that each of them recognized that beyond the circumstances of birth and color and social class, each of them shared a very human pain, the pain of losing a child. For in that moment of shared pain, they discovered that beyond all differences, both apparent and real, there was one point at which they were absolutely the same. They were both made in the image of God, and from that fundamental point of identity, they could begin to love each other. And when they recognized their common identity and felt those first stirrings of love for each other, they began to know the truth, and the truth began to set them free. Freedom for the young white woman came in the form of courage to work within the limitations of her own condition, to stop the abusive treatment of the slaves by her mother-in-law and plantation overseer. Freedom for the young slave woman came in the form of courage to hang on and do what she had to do to secure the promise from her master that the son she had borne him would be a free man and not a slave.

Today is Reformation Sunday. We remember, with thanksgiving, the rediscovery of the freedom of God's children by a 16th century Augustinian monk named Martin Luther. At a time when much of the church had forgotten the simple, yet profound truth that sets human beings free to love and live in relationship to God, overlaying that truth with the weight of dogmas and elaborate systems of merits and indulgences, Luther found a gracious God. He found a God who was committed to human freedom, and who required nothing of us but that we ground ourselves in our relationship to him, trusting in his love for us, continuing in his word and letting his word shine through the love we show toward others.

This is still the way to freedom. If you are struggling with a life out of control, driven by forces you don't understand, if you are a seeker after truth but haven't found it, your struggle and your quest can end here. "If the Son makes you free, you shall be free indeed."

All Saints' Sunday (C)
Luke 6:20-31

The Politics
Of The Saints

During the last presidential election, you may have seen the comic strip "Frank and Earnest" where Frank is sitting on an airplane with a worried look on his face, and he asks the stewardess, "Are there any air bags on this plane?" She replies, "There are a couple of congressmen up in first class."

By the time the presidential election campaign wound down to its final hours, most of us were eagerly looking forward to a little relief from listening to the air bags. All those speeches that said nothing. All those hours of prime-time television advertising. Really the whole thing could have been carried out much more efficiently. Each of the candidates could have boiled down all their windy rhetoric to one simple slogan. President Bush, for instance, could have just gotten up in front of the television cameras and said, "Taxes and trust." Governor Clinton could then have had his moment in the limelight and said, "Time for change." Then Ross Perot could have come forward and yelled "Deficit!" Think of how much time and money and energy we could have all saved. It's no wonder politics has such a bad name.

The reality is, however, that there's no part of life that is not concerned with politics. I'm not talking about this partisan orgy of mud-slinging and rhetorical hype that we call a presidential election. Nor am I speaking of politics as the arena of public life which is concerned with government. That's politics in the narrow sense. I'm talking about something much more basic.

Politics is about people and the relationships between people or groups of people. The word politics comes from the Greek word *polis* which means city, or its derivative *politeuma* which meals commonwealth. Politics has to do with the way in which we live in society and order our lives for the common weal or good. Life itself is political, and there is virtually no decision I can make, nothing I can say, no action that I take that does not have political consequences, for I do not live in isolation from other people. When I sneeze, my neighbor catches cold.

So the question becomes not will I be political, but what kind of politics will I practice? How will my words or my actions or my decisions affect the lives of other people around me? What message will I be sending? The same question applies to groups and organizations as well as to individuals.

All Saints' Sunday is a good time to think about politics in this broader sense. For on All Saints', we take time to remember that Christians are not isolated individuals who live in this world alone, passing through it untouched by anyone or anything and not having any impact or effect on anyone. We are a people, a *politeuma*, a commonwealth. We're connected. We affect each other and we affect the world around us in so many ways.

On All Saints', we also pause to remember those of our *politeuma*, those fellow-citizens of the household of God, who are no longer present among us in body, but whose memory we hold dear and who have now joined that larger city, that larger *politeuma* toward which we are all travelling, and in which we already hold citizenship, the New Jerusalem, the City of God.

In remembering those of our fellowship who have died in the past year, we also call to mind their impact upon us, and our own impact, as the people of God, on the world around us. In other words, we consider our politics.

It would be impossible to listen to the words of Jesus as recorded in our gospel lessons and not realize their political impact. The stately and dignified language of our English translations which make for suitable reading in public worship can sometimes camouflage the raw impact of the words themselves. "Blessed are you poor," sounds somehow pious and dignified. But we lose the ironic force, and even the gallows humor present in the words themselves. "Congratulations you poor, for yours is the domain of God" would get us much closer to the real spirit of Jesus' words. "Congratulations you who are hungry now for your turn is coming to be filled. Congratulations you who weep now, for your time of laughter and joy is coming. But woe to you who are rich; you've already gotten all you're ever going to get. Woe to you who are full now, for your own day of hunger is coming. Woe to you who are laughing now, for sorrow and pain is just around the corner."

Who can deny the shocking impact of those words? Who could deny their political implications? Imagine yourself in the audience who heard Jesus say those things. How would you hear them? If you were one of the poor or hungry or mourning, perhaps you would be cynical of the promises in Jesus words. "Sure," you might reply. "Another politician telling me how lucky I am to be poor." Or perhaps you would be moved with revolutionary fervor. "Right on!" you would shout. "The revolution is coming." But if you were a comfortable, well-fed, hard-working middle-class person with a good job, a house with your mortgage nearly paid off, and good health, those words would have a very different impact, wouldn't they? They might be rather unsettling, causing you to feel some guilt or some sense of unease. They might plant a small seed of doubt in your mind, that maybe your comfortable life is really a house of cards that could come tumbling down without warning. Or they might be highly offensive. "Why doesn't somebody shut this guy up?" might be your reaction. Well, in Jesus' case, somebody did. Jesus was not crucified because he poked some mild fun at the religious establishment or because he did some good things for people like curing their illnesses. People don't crucify stand-up comics or faith-healers or even mild social critics. People who get crucified are people who are perceived as threats, as dangerous subversives. The Romans crucified Jesus because they feared him as a political subversive. They recognized that the politics of his words and deeds had the potential for overturning their world.

What would happen if there existed a significant group of people within any society, who suddenly began to preach that we should love our enemies and do good to them and pray for them, and actually began to do that? It sounds good, doesn't it? Well, I suppose it depends on where you sit whether it sounds good or not. If you're the CEO of a major defense contractor, I doubt if you'd welcome much talk about loving our enemies. That's a very political issue, isn't it? And what would happen to our entire banking industry and the stock market, the whole foundation of our economy, if suddenly there were a significant group of people who preached and practiced lending to others without charging interest, and even without forcing them to repay the loan? Would that turn the world upside down or what? Do you wonder that Jesus was crucified?

John Howard Yoder, a Mennonite theologian, wrote a well-known book back in the early '80s called *The Politics of Jesus* in which he explored some of these very issues. Those of us who call ourselves followers of Jesus cannot get away from the fact that following Jesus means practicing a particular kind of politics — the politics of love, of non-violence, of non-retaliation, of generosity, of mercy. And that brand of politics will set us squarely against the grain of a world which practices a very different brand of politics. The world says "The strong survive, the weak perish." It's the law of nature, and we make it the law of society. Christian politics says, "The strong have an obligation to defend and protect the interests of the weak, so that the weak become strong." We don't practice survival of the fittest, but care for the neediest. The world's politics says, "Grab all you can and hang on to it." The politics of Jesus says, "From anyone who wishes to take away your coat, do not withhold even your shirt." The politics of the world says, "An eye for an eye, and a tooth for a tooth." The politics of Jesus says, "If someone strikes you on one cheek, turn the other to him also." The world says, "You've got to look out for Number One, and devil take the hindmost." Jesus says, "Be merciful, even as your Father is merciful."

That's a pretty tough program, isn't it? These words of Jesus are very hard for us to hear. Even harder for us to put into practice. Maybe if we were all Mother Teresas, we could, but we're just ordinary Joes and Sallys. We're just trying to provide for our families, get our kids educated, live a decent life, and do as much good along the way as we can, but we're not heroes. We're not Mother Teresa or Joan of Arc or Saint Francis of Assisi. We're not saints.

Ah, but we are! That's precisely how Paul and other writers in the New Testament refer to the Christian community — as "the saints." The word saint means "holy one," and the word holy doesn't mean especially pious or religious or heroic. The word holy means "set apart." It means "called out from." It means "distinctive." We are God's distinctive people. We are God's called out ones. Or as the older English versions translated it, "God's peculiar people." Well, it is pretty peculiar to practice the politics of Jesus — to return good for evil, blessing for curse, generosity for selfishness, liberality for greed, mercy for ruthlessness. The words of the song that many of us have sung say it in one line: "They'll know we are Christians by our love." That's us, or at least, that's what we're called to be — saints, peculiar people, people set apart by their practice of the politics of love.

Perhaps that's why on All Saints' Sunday, we don't primarily remember the great heroes and heroines of the faith, but we remember the ordinary Christians who have been part of our own company of saints. We remember how they struggled to live faithfully; we remember their gifts which they offered to the service of Christ and to the rest of God's people. We member their humility, their love, their service. And in remembering them, we find courage and faith to try, however difficult it may be, to be faithful ourselves in practicing the politics of Jesus.

We're not under any illusions that we always get it right. Nor do we think it's easy to practice the politics of love. In fact, we know that it is sometimes the hardest thing of all — to love another person or to love a whole group of persons for Christ's sake. The cost can sometimes be very high. We may be exploited or misunderstood. We may stir up resentment or frustration. We may risk being trampled on. Nothing is harder in this world than loving others, particularly those who are enemies or strangers or aliens. It's not natural. But it is what saints do, or try to do, and that's why we need to do it together, why we must do it together. We can never do it alone.

Being a people set apart usually means being a people in conflict with the values and structures of the world around us. In the closing lines of George Bernard Shaw's play *Saint Joan,* the story of Joan of Arc, a ghostly Joan who has just discovered the church has made her a saint some four centuries after that same church had burned her as a heretic, prays, "O God, who madest this beautiful earth, when will it be ready for thy saints?" Anytime we really set out to live the politics of Jesus in this world, we're bound to wonder the same thing. Is our distinctiveness having any effect? Is it worth the energy, the risk, the dangers of always swimming against the current? Is the world ready for love?

The people for whom the visions in the Book of Daniel were written were wondering the same thing. They are trying to live faithfully and yet the powers of evil seem to grow stronger. Daniel's vision offers them a new perspective on their situation. It lets them see that there is a deeper dimension to reality than what meets the eye. By faith and hope, they can grasp it. It can only be described in visionary language. But it's no less real for that. Most of the great truths can only be described in figures of speech. The seer, in his vision, sees one like a Son of Adam, a human being, coming on the clouds with power and glory, and a voice from heaven tells him the meaning of this vision. "The saints of the most High shall receive the kingdom, and they shall possess the kingdom for ever and ever" (Daniel 7:18). That same ability to grasp by faith and hope what is hidden from our eyes is what is necessary to penetrate those ironic and powerfully political truths of Jesus. It takes faith and hope to see the poor as possessing the kingdom of God, the hungry satisfied, and the mourners rejoicing. This is not a promise of pie-in-the-sky-by-and-by; rather it is a description of what is real and true. It is a call to obedience and action; to live in the light of God's truth, in the light of God's reality; to practice the politics of God's domain even in the midst of the politics of this world. And when we dare to take the risks such action demands, we discover that what we have grasped in faith and hope, is, in fact, the only solid foundation under our lives.

And so we gather around the table to remember who we are — God's *politeuma*, God's commonwealth. We gather to recommit ourselves to practice the politics of heaven in the midst of this world. We gather to eat and drink the bread and wine of heaven to gain strength for the rigors that follow that calling will bring upon us. And we remember those faithful ones who have gone ahead of us to that domain of God where faith is swallowed up in sight, where what we see only in hope and by visions, they see face to face.

All Saints' Sunday (L, RC)
Matthew 5:1-12
Revelation 7:9-17 (Second Lesson reference)

Remembering The Saints

There was a column in the *New York Times* on Wednesday, October 28, 1992, by Robertson Davies titled "Haunted By Halloween." After tracing the origins of Halloween to the ancient Celtic festival of the Death of the Year, and showing how the Christian church piggybacked the Feast of All Saints onto this pagan festival which marked both the death of the sun at the beginning of winter and the remembrance of their dead ancestors, Davies argued for a recovery of the best part of the ancient Halloween — the remembrance of the dead.

> Let us recognize that we are not the ultimate triumph but rather that we are beads on a string. Let us behave with decency to the beads that were strung before us, and hope modestly that the beads that come after us will not hold us of no account because we are dead ... What might we profitably do on Halloween? Look backward, and consider those who went before us. The road ahead is inevitably dark, but to see where we have been may offer unexpected hints about who we are and where we should be heading. Triviality about the past leads certainly toward a trivial future.

John Wesley, the 18th century founder of Methodism, said that the Feast of All Saints was his favorite festival in the church year. It was the one time, more than at any other, when the great chain of witness, from the earliest worshippers of the God of Abraham, Isaac and Jacob, was emphasized and brought into the present through remembrance. I think it's my favorite too. On All Saints' Sunday, more than at any other time, I feel surrounded by a great cloud of witnesses.

That wonderful, magnificent passage from the Book of Revelation which is our epistle lesson (Revelation 7:9-17), and which some of us can never hear without wanting to sing it as Handel set it to music in *The Messiah,* is a passage of remembrance of the heroic witnesses to the faith. Psychologists tell us that our memories are what form our sense of identity. Events and persons which do not stick in our memories really do not influence us much at all. The things and persons we remember, however, have the power to shape us and mold us and direct us long after they are past and gone, even when those memories are deeply buried in our subconscious mind. To a large extent, we are what we remember. I don't mean primarily the kind of remembering that we do when we're cramming for an exam, and we try to make dates and times and equations stick in our heads long enough to regurgitate them for the professor, or the kind of remembering we do when our husband or wife says, "Honey, don't forget to stop for milk on your way home." I'm speaking of remembering in a much deeper sense.

A Methodist pastor had lunch with an Episcopal priest with whom he had gone to college 25 years earlier, and whom he hadn't seen or kept in touch with all those years. They didn't talk about anything serious; they just remembered together. Through their memories, they relived their college days, names of significant people came up, and with their names came faces and voices and a reaffirmation of what those people had meant to them for good or for ill. And with that remembrance of things past came a deeper level of understanding of who they were now, compared with who they had been back then. We've probably all had similar experiences. And the strange thing is that when we do this kind of significant remembering of the persons in the past who have had important influences on us, we begin to get a sense of our place in the world, and a hint or a glimpse of where we might be headed. In short, memory leads to hope.

And that's what's happening in this passage from the Revelation. The seer is writing to seven congregations in Asia Minor somewhere near the end of the first century and the beginning of the second. In the 50 or 60 years since Jesus was crucified, the new movement of people who believed that he had been raised from death had spread significantly over the whole Roman Empire, as far west as Gaul, or what is now France and Spain. Christians made up a significant block of the population and were recognized as (potentially at least) a powerful political force. This made the emperor Domitian a bit edgy, and to make sure he was able to hold the empire together, large and unwieldy as it was, he instituted a kind of pledge of allegiance, similar in intent to our own pledge of allegiance to the flag, but with more serious repercussions. In Domitian's version, however, subject people as well as Roman citizens were required to offer, once a year in one of the temples of the state religion, a sacrifice to the divine genius of the emperor. Failure to do so constituted treason, and was punishable by imprisonment, exile, or even death. Domitian didn't really believe he was divine; the doctrine of the emperor's divinity was a political doctrine. If the emperor was descended from the gods, then his rule was legitimized.

And since most of the Christians were cosmopolitan peoples of the Graeco-Roman world, the emperor figured he could ensure their loyalty by making them say the pledge of allegiance. Was he ever in for a surprise! First of all, he discovered, they were as devoted to the worship of their God Christus as the Jews ever were to theirs. But when they were threatened with exile or even death for refusing to take the oath of loyalty, they reacted in a very surprising way. They didn't revolt or use their numbers to create political instability by preaching insurrection. Instead, they willingly walked to the stake to be burned, or into the arenas where the lions waited, singing praises to their God and speaking words of forgiveness to their persecutors. They became martyrs.

The word "martyr" literally means witness. Their witness to their faith in Christ was so strong, so potent, that they willingly went to their deaths rather than compromise with a state which they believed was making illegitimate demands upon them.

And so, to these Christians who were living through a time of great ordeal, John, one of their pastors who had been exiled to a penal colony in the Aegean Sea, wrote this visionary letter to them. By adopting this visionary style of literature, he invites them to use their imaginations to glimpse a different reality above and beyond the grim time of testing which confronts them on an almost daily basis. He lets them see what's really going on, if only they could eavesdrop on God holding court in heaven. As they feel the flames begin to lick around their feet at the stake, or hear the roars of the hungry lions, they can take hope that above and behind and within this terrible ordeal, there is a different reality. He calls to their remembrance the example of faithful people who have witnessed to their faith in God without flinching, and he turns their eyes toward the future when they will be part of that great innumerable throng from every nation, tribe and the language, who stand around the throne of God singing "Blessing and glory and wisdom and thanks and honor and power and might be to our God forever and ever!" The memory of past faithful ones will inspire them to faithfulness in their own time of ordeal and cement the bond which binds the whole people of God, past, present, and future, into one vast and thrilling community of worship. And this remembrance will renew and strengthen them in hope.

Robertson Davies was right about our need to remember our dead — those who have gone before us. What sense of family solidarity can we have if we do not remember our fathers and mothers, our grandparents and great-grandparents who have made such an impact on our lives? And if it is so important to our sense of identity to remember our biological families, how vital is it also that we remember our ancestors in faith? How can we hope to know how our faith relates to the present circumstances we face if we know nothing of how that faith gave hope and meaning to others who have gone before us? We Americans, perhaps more so than any other people on earth, lack a strong and vital historical memory. We live totally in the present divorced from the past and with little hope in the future. We don't remember, and so we cannot understand who we are and where we are going or what we are becoming.

And this American penchant for loss of memory creeps over into our churches and religious life as well. We ignore, actually devalue, what generations of Christians have learned about God before us. We are ignorant of theology, ignorant of the great tradition of spirituality and worship which has preceded us, content often to live only for the spiritual impulses of the moment. We don't know that we stand upon the shoulders of giants, and that if we can see any glimpse of God at all, it is only because there have been faithful witnesses who have helped us see, and who are now part of that great throng singing praises to the Lamb who is in the center of the throne of God.

These giants of faith upon whose shoulders we stand are not necessarily those whom the world would acknowledge as giants. A few are Paul, whose grasp of the mind of Christ has never been equalled; Augustine; Thomas Aquinas; Theresa of Avila; Lady Julian of Norwich; Martin Luther; John Wesley and his faithful mother Susanna; the saintly Japanese Christian Kagawa or Mother Teresa of Calcutta — these and a relatively few others have attracted notice beyond their immediate circumstances and helped shape the faith of thousands or even millions.

But most of the giants of faith have been people, who for the most part were unheralded and unknown, except to those whose lives they personally touched and to whom they gave hope. They are those quiet saints who have visibly manifested the qualities Jesus pronounced blessed in the Beatitudes —

poverty of spirit, humility, purity of heart, mercy, hunger for justice, and peacemakers.

Today is a day for remembering the faithful witnesses in our own spiritual family tree. A friend told me of the influence of his great-grandmother, whom he doubted he would find it very easy to really like if she were still alive. She was the epitome of a dour, ultra-strict Scots-Irish Protestant who didn't have the greatest sense of humor in the world. But she did have a passionate love for God and a wonderful and powerful life of prayer. One of my friend's earliest memories is from the time when he was about three or four years old, his parents were away and he was sleeping at Great-grandma's house. He remembers waking up frightened in the middle of the night because it was dark and he could hear voices. But he discovered it was Gram, down on her knees beside the bed praying fervently for some missionary that her church supported. In the morning, she told him that God had awakened her from sleep and told her to pray for such and such a missionary. And she said that this happened very often. When he asked how God spoke to her, she just said that the thought came clearly into her mind, and she just knew she was supposed to pray. So pray she did. And as my friend grew older, he understood that this was just a normal part of his great-grandmother's life. She probably spent more time in the middle of the night on her knees than in bed asleep. But letters would come from missionaries all over the world, telling of some experience where they were in need or in trouble, and were assured by that same inner voice that she was praying for them, and it gave them courage and hope. Her example of intercessory prayer inspired her daughter-in-law to similarly pray for not only the missionaries, but for each of her children and grandchildren every day of her life, and her granddaughter still never lets a day go without spending some significant time on her knees in prayer for her three sons who are pastors and for all her nephews and nieces and cousins who are in ministry.

Today is a day for all of us to remember the saints, all the saints who have trod the path of faithfulness to God before us, and especially those whom we have personally encountered on our journey, whose witness to their faith has contributed so much to our own. When we gather around the Lord's table, we gather to remember in this deep sense: we eat and drink the bread and wine in remembrance of Jesus. And by remembering, we recall his life into ours to help us know who we are and what the meaning of our journey is, and we learn to trust him to lead us into the future. But we don't gather alone; we are part of the communion of saints. And those words that we say at the beginning of the Great Thanksgiving as we gather around the Lord's table, ring in our hearts with new meaning, "And so, with your people on earth, and all the company of heaven we praise your name, and join their unending hymn ...." That's who we're in fellowship with this morning — all the saints in earth and heaven, who by their faithful witness to Jesus Christ, offer us the priceless gift of hope.

Proper 27
Pentecost 25
Ordinary Time 32
Luke 20:27-38

The Importance Of Asking The Right Questions

A clergy colleague has made it a policy for many years to refer what he calls "six-year-old theology questions" to his wife. Since she has taught very young children for many years, she has a much better grasp than he does of how to address the real concerns in questions which little kids ask. The other day, a first-grader brought a picture with him into her class where she teaches English as a second language. He had found it in the trash basket in another class. It was a drawing of a skeleton, titled "Inside of Me." It was designed to teach children that everyone has a skeleton inside of them. He unfolded it proudly and showed it to the class. One little girl from India was astounded at the thought that she and others had this scary-looking skeleton inside them, and so she pressed the issue a bit farther. "Even you got one of these inside you, Mrs. K?" The teacher replied, "Yes, I have one too." The next question was the theological one. "Even God got one inside him?" Now in a class made up of children from many different countries, cultures, and religious backgrounds (most of them not Christians), you can imagine that this question had the potential for major theological debate. I doubt if I'd have had the presence of mind to give the answer my friend's wife did; but, as usual, her expertise in six-year-old theology saved the day. "If God needs a skeleton, I'm sure he has one," she replied.

"God has everything he needs." This apparently satisfied the theological curiosity of the class, and they got on with the lesson.

Asking questions is an essential part of learning. If we don't know something, we look for someone who does and we ask. The only dumb question is the one you don't ask because you think it's a dumb question. We learn by asking questions about what we don't know.

While no question is a dumb question if it is designed to help you acquire knowledge or information which you don't currently have, there are questions which are the wrong questions to ask, and which, if asked, will actually prevent us from learning what we need to know.

We see two examples of these kinds of questions in our lessons this morning. In the prophecy of Zechariah, we're told that the people came to the prophet to ask a question. About 50 years earlier, in 587 B.C., the Babylonian empire had conquered Judea, destroying Jerusalem and the temple of God. The leading citizens were then carried off into exile. For the people who remained in the land of Palestine during the 70 years before the Exiles came back, the memory of the devastation of their holy city and the temple of God was a powerful political force uniting the people. Since the temple had been destroyed in the fifth month of the year and the governor of Jerusalem executed in the seventh month, every year thereafter, the people fasted and mourned during the fifth and seventh months. In this way, they based their lives on the memory of the destruction they had suffered in the past.

The question that the people come to the prophets to ask is this, "Now that 50 or so years have passed, and the Babylonians have been defeated by the Persians, should we continue to fast and mourn in the fifth and seventh months?" Now that sounds like a harmless enough question, doesn't it? They're a little confused by the change of administrations, and they're not quite sure of how to proceed. Change the words "Bablyonian" and "Persian" to "Republicans" and "Democrats," and suddenly the question seems surprisingly contemporary.

But the answer they get from the prophet is not the answer they were expecting.

The answer to their question is itself a question — from God! "Then the word of the Lord of hosts came to me: Say to all the people of the land and the priests: When you fasted and lamented in the fifth month and in the seventh, was it for me that you fasted? And when you eat and when you drink, do you not eat and drink only for yourselves?" (Zechariah 7:4-7).

Their question is a self-serving question. It does not arise out of a desire to know the truth, to gain knowledge of God's will, but out of a desire to get God's sanction on their own national pity-party. They want God to bless their long-nurtured resentments, to sanction their long-standing hatred of those who destroyed their temple and holy city. Every year, when they fast on the fifth and seventh months, they are, in effect, saying, "This is who we are: We're the people who were beaten up by the Babylonians. Now this new administration had come, and we're not sure we want to change. We've grown comfortable with our identity; we like our fasts and our mourning and our moaning about the good old days. Can't we keep on doing this?"

But God let them know in no uncertain terms that they had asked the wrong question. "Was it for me you fasted? No, you did it for yourselves. Your concern was not with what I require of you, but with your own agenda. Your religion is a religion designed to make yourself feel better, not a religion designed to please God and enable you to do what God requires. And then comes God's pointed commands about the sort of religion he's really interested in: "Render true judgments, show kindness and mercy to one another; do not oppress the widow, the orphan, the alien, or the poor; and do not devise evil in your hearts against one another" (Zechariah 7:9-10). The clear implication is that while they piously fasted and mourned to commemorate the oppression and injustice which they suffered at the hands of a foreign nation, they themselves practiced oppression within their own nation against all those who were without power or an advocate.

When we ask the wrong question, in this case, a self-serving question, we shouldn't be surprised if we get an answer that we neither expect nor wish to hear. Our question becomes a judgment upon us. Like the people of ancient Judea, if we are going to find our way forward as a nation, we are going to have to stop asking questions that serve only our own individual or parochial interests and start asking the larger questions about truth, justice, kindness, mercy, and meeting needs that may be more pressing than our own.

In God's world, there is no true security for those who are unwilling to risk themselves and their own comfort for the sake of kindness, mercy, justice, and truth. All such comfort is false comfort. It is the comfort of the dead. Real life is life on the edge, always at risk, always vulnerable, always demanding that we live by faith and not by sight. That we live by trust in God rather than trust in our bank account. That we live by hope rather than by achievement. That we live for others rather than for ourselves.

The Sadducees who came to Jesus brought a similar kind of question. Their question is an attack question. It's a question designed to destroy the other person's viewpoint so that one's own viewpoint wins without ever having to be defended. Its purpose, like the other, is to prevent them from having to change. The Sadducees weren't really interested in what Jesus believed about the possibility of resurrection from the dead. Their question about one bride for seven brothers was not a question which they hoped would bring them some new knowledge or understanding. They already knew that the law which obligated a man to marry his brother's widow and raise up children by her which would legally be his dead brother's children was a compassionate social custom designed to provide for people who had no voice or standing in that culture — widows — and to ensure the continuity of a family's line. They didn't need to be instructed on the meaning and significance of levirate marriage. Their question was not serious, except that it was seriously designed to entrap Jesus into taking a position that would alienate people while making themselves look good at his expense.

We're familiar with questions like that, aren't we? We've all used these sorts of questions from time to time, haven't we — the question designed not to bring us closer to the truth, but to demolish the other person's point of view so that we protect ourselves from having to change our own behavior or cherished ideas.

But Jesus' opponents are the ones who are demolished by their own questions. He cuts through to the real issue — do they really believe in God? Is their God big enough and powerful enough to raise the dead? His God is. The God of Abraham, Isaac, and Jacob is. God is a God of the living. And people of faith, whether long dead or not, are alive to this God, who is the author not of death but of life.

This business of learning to ask the right questions applies not only to our national life, but to every area of life. It applies to our life as a church, certainly. If we are always asking the question, "What should we do so that we will not have to give up the things we've become comfortable doing?" we will never become what God wants us to be and we will not experience the very security we seek.

At a church-growth workshop the leader, Bill Easum, who himself grew a church from 29 members to over 2,400 members, said that too often the questions churches ask themselves are questions that are motivated by a desire to maintain whatever is comfortable. That's why some wag has said that the seven last words of the church are "We've never done it that way before." Bill Easum spoke of the three greatest sins of the church, and one of them was, "We're more in love with our traditions than we are with our missions." If we are intent on preserving the patterns of church life we've grown comfortable with, we'll soon discover that God has moved on and left us behind. God is always out there ahead of us, leading us into the future, and if we want to be working hand in hand with God, we have to be willing to ask the right questions. Not, "What can we do to preserve what we find comfortable?" but "What can we do to be partners with God in mission?" The first question leads to a church that is dead and declining; the second to a church that is alive and dynamic.

The same is true in our personal lives as well. How often we settle for what's comfortable instead of what is true and life-giving. It takes no effort, demands no sacrifice, involves no risk to simply go along with what the world says is important at any moment. It takes no courage, no commitment, no faith to just go on doing what we've been doing. To go on working 60- and 70-hour weeks to provide for our family's material comfort, and watch our families go down the drain because we're too busy working to be present for them. It's easier even to live with our addictions and compulsions than it is to confront and overcome them. Healing is hard work, and frequently, it is very painful work as well. Yet without the willingness to get out of the comfort zone, healing cannot come.

The poet T. S. Eliot in his famous poem "The Wasteland," calls April the "cruelest month," because the showers of April stir up the dull and dormant roots of trees and flowers to begin bursting forth with new life instead of allowing them to remain comfortably asleep in the frozen ground of winter. Yet the sleep of tree roots and flower bulbs is the sleep of hibernation, not of rest. Trees were meant to put out green leaves; tulips were meant to push up through the soil and produce beautiful blossoms. Human beings are also meant to grow, to mature, to blossom, not to hibernate in the frozen sleep of habit or tradition or familiarity. Paul says that we were meant to grow until "we attain to the full height of the stature of Christ."

And that's often the point of our fear. We're more afraid of change, more afraid of growth, than we are of becoming stuck in our present level of development. Better a comfortable rut than the risks of the journey. Yet God is a God of the living, not of the dead. God is always there nudging us to get out of our ruts, to leave false comfort and security behind, and take the risks of faith by following him into the future. The future is only frightening if God is not there ahead of us. If God is there, then what do we have to fear? What looks from our angle like a risky business — growing, moving on, living by faith rather than by sight — from another angle is the safest of all possible places to be, in God's company.

At every level of life, our personal life where we seek fulfillment and meaning, our life as a church seeking to be faithful in our mission, and our life as a nation seeking to move into the future, we must ask the right questions if we're going to discover something more than the false comfort of the status quo, if we're going to discover where God is actively stirring dull roots into new life. We must learn to ask not, "What should we do so that we can be most comfortable, so that we will not have to be changed?" but "Where must we go, what must we do, to find our true life in God?"

Proper 28
Pentecost 26
Ordinary Time 33
Luke 21:5-19

Not Yet Quitting Time

You may remember reading or hearing of the Korean Christian group who predicted that Christ was going to return on October 28, 1992, all Christians would be taken to heaven, and the rest of the world would enter the terrible catastrophes of the end times. Well, we're still here, and unless you count the presidential election which was held a month later as a terrible apocalyptic catastrophe, I don't see that the ordinary catastrophes were much worse than usual.

There's nothing new in this miscalculation of what we have come to call the second coming or the second advent of Christ. For centuries, Christians, especially those who belong to sectarian groups, have been attempting to use the scriptures to calculate the timing of the second coming, and always without success. This practice began extremely early. Even within our New Testament, for example in Paul's first letter to the Thessalonians, which was written only about ten years after Jesus' crucifixion, we see an attempt to come to terms with this expectation. Almost from the moment the earliest Christians became convinced that Jesus had been raised from the dead by the power of God, they began looking for him to return to earth in power and glory to establish the eternal kingdom of God.

Much of the attractiveness of doing this sort of calculation arises from feelings that the world is getting worse instead of better, and that wickedness is increasing, and a conviction that there's no hope of things getting better when the bad people seem to outnumber God's people. That sense of alienation and fear and weariness with fighting what seems like a futile battle for righteousness is what leads to a fascination with the end of the world. The tragic and violent end of the Branch Davidian cult in Waco, Texas, came about, in part, because of the cult's obsession with the sense that the world was soon coming to an end.

If we were to be asked for a favorite or familiar passage of scripture, I daresay that none of us here would name any of the lessons we've heard this morning. They're a bit strange, aren't they, to say the least. All of them in one way or another, have the end of the world in view.

The prophet Malachi declares his vision of the final day of the Lord, "See, the day is coming, burning like an oven" (Malachi 4:1), and he describes that day as being both a day of judgment and of salvation. For the wicked it will come as judgment. For the righteous, it will be the rising of the "sun of righteousness with healing in its wings" (Malachi 4:2). Same day. But how it is experienced will be determined by the character of those who experience it. For those who live heedlessly, selfishly, unmindful of God, disobedient to God's will, it will be experienced as a "burning oven," in which all that is not good will perish. For those who live in faithfulness to God, who do God's will rather than their own, it will come as a day of salvation and blessing and healing.

In the community of Christians in Thessalonica, there were those who became so convinced that the time was short, that they figured, what's the point of continuing to work. We'll just stay in church all day, we'll join in the covered-dish suppers, we'll sing hymns, we'll pray together, we'll have good fellowship and enjoy ourselves while we wait for Jesus to come back and deliver us from this evil world.

But the writer of the epistle sharply reprimands them for this attitude, "Keep away from believers who are living in idleness and not according to the tradition they received from us" (2 Thessalonians 3:6), he tells them. He's not speaking about lazy people in general. He's speaking particularly to people who, probably because they were lazy people to begin with, are using the hope of the soon return of Christ as an excuse to stop working and sponge off the rest of the Christian community. He exhorts them to straighten up, get back to work, and follow his own example and teaching which was, "If you don't work, you don't eat." And his concluding remark on this subject is "Brothers and sisters, do not be weary in welldoing" (2 Thessalonians 3:13) — in doing what is right.

In our gospel lesson, we find Jesus saying something very similar to his followers. In Luke's community, there were apparently some who misinterpreted the hard times they were going through, especially the persecutions that sometimes broke out against the Christians as they strove for official recognition and tolerance as a bona fide religion in the eyes of the Roman imperial power. But Luke is concerned that they not interpret a time of severe trial as a sign of the imminent end, and just give up hope and give up their mission of spreading the Gospel of Christ. So in his story, we see Jesus warning his followers that they should not interpret their troubles or the world's troubles as signs that the end is upon them. Rather, he tells them, "This will be an opportunity for you to testify ... I will give you words and a wisdom that none of your opponents will be able to withstand or contradict. It's true that some of you will suffer betrayal by family and friends, and some of you will even be put to death. But don't worry, not a hair of your heads will be harmed."

Easy for him to say. Don't you just love the absurdity of that statement, "Some of you will be put to death, but don't worry because not a hair of your heads will be harmed"? Of course it's easy for him to say, if you take those words as the words of the risen Jesus to his church. For the risen Jesus has experienced that very paradoxical, seemingly absurd truth. He was put to death, but death did not ultimately harm him.

God raised him from the dead, the God whose word creates life where there is no life. So viewed from this side of Jesus' resurrection, those words contain, not an absurdity, but a profound truth. The follower of Jesus is someone who can be faithful, even in the face of death, because he or she knows that even death can work no ultimate harm.

Now, most of us aren't sitting around thinking about the second coming of Christ all the time like those early Christians in Luke's community or in Thessalonica. If, after nearly 2,000 years, no one has successfully calculated the date of the second advent, it's probably because we were never intended to occupy ourselves with such pursuits in the first place. To ask when or how is to ask the wrong question. But some of us may have fallen into the opposite error of thinking that because we cannot calculate the day and the hour of the end, or because the end hasn't come in all this time, there isn't any end at all. And that's a more deadly error than the error of focusing on the when and the how.

For if the New Testament is clear on anything, it is that the end has already begun. It began when God raised Jesus from the dead and exalted him as Lord of all. The completion of the end will come in God's good time, a time we cannot calculate, but which is nevertheless guaranteed. Jesus' resurrection is the first installment, the down-payment if you will, of the full re-creation of the world.

So the question for us is not "When will that day come?" nor "What will be the manner of its coming?" nor even "Will it ever come at all?" but rather "In view of the certainty of that day's coming, how should we live?"

And the answer to that question is to live in faithfulness to God. All three of our lessons agree on that answer. In faithfulness to God. In obedience to God's will. In bearing faithful witness before "kings and governors" for Jesus' sake. It is not becoming weary in doing what is right.

But that's just the rub, isn't it? It's not that we dispute the answer. We all know the answer. We've known it for as long as we've been Christians most of us. We don't doubt it. We know that we're to be faithful, to be righteous, to do what is right, to do good. And if we're mature Christians, we know also that we can't do good without the power of the Holy Spirit working within us to give us both the will and the ability to do what is right. Our doing what is right is not our achievement, but Christ's achievement within us and through us. That's what grace is: God giving to us what we need to do what God requires us to do, quite apart from any achievement or qualification of our own.

But the problem for many of us is that we get weary in well-doing. We get tired. It's hard to be faithful all the time, isn't it? It's tough to always pay attention to the needs of others more than we pay attention to our own needs and wants. It's tough to volunteer to staff a homeless shelter or feed the hungry or teach at Bible club for children from the housing projects, or to serve faithfully on the administrative board or to teach a Sunday school class and to keep on doing it week after week after week, year after year after year. It's tough, not only to give our time and energy to do these things which we know are right, but to be expected to pay for the privilege of doing them as well. It's burn-out city.

It's also tough to always try to do what is right even in our personal lives and within our families, isn't it? It's really hard to be honest all the time when it seems like we'd get ahead faster if we cut some corners. It's tough to be charitable to colleagues who'd just as soon stick a knife in our backs as not. It's hard to be committed to the causes and practices that we know are right, when it seems like we're fighting an uphill battle. We get tired. I know I do. And my family knows I do. And my friends know I do. They often pay the price when I'm tired. They get short answers, the defensive reactions, the irritable response. Maybe if we always get stroked and rewarded for doing what is right, it wouldn't be so bad, but as those disciples of Jesus discovered, they were more likely to be persecuted. Wouldn't it be so much easier to avoid becoming weary in well-doing if we could look forward to a pat on the back instead of a kick in the behind for our efforts? Or what's even worse, just taken for granted. To a group of conscientious and overworked people, the exhortation, "Do not be weary in well-doing," just adds another burden to our already over-burdened lives.

But it's just at the point of our weariness, just at the point where we're ready to quit, where our energy is all used up and burned out, that we need that vision of the approaching end to sustain us. Just as a long-distance runner needs to keep the image of the finish line in her mind in order to summon up the stamina to finish the race, or a woman in labor needs to keep her mind on the new life to come to enable her to endure her travail, so we need the truth of the second advent to enable us to run our race with patience and hope and endurance. It's not yet quitting time. The road is long, the way is hard, we will get tired to the point of exhaustion, but the end is in view, Christ is the Lord of history, and in God's good time, the end will come — an end that is really a new beginning. We may not be able to see the future in detail, but we can see the large outlines. That future means life from the dead, for us and for the whole creation. That future means that ultimately human greed and human evil and human selfishness will not have the last word. Paul says, "We are saved in hope." And he's exactly right. Not hope that is mere wishful thinking, but hope that is anchored in a firm trust in the God who raised Jesus from the dead, and who keeps his promise to his creation. That's why we must never, never lose sight of the end, that day of which the prophet Malachi, and Jesus, and Paul all spoke. They themselves lived in light of that day, and it colored all that they did and suffered and endured. It was their polestar, the fixed point by which they navigated. And it's the fixed point by which we must navigate as well if we are not to become weary in well-doing. Only hope in the final triumph of God will enable us to keep on doing what is right, despite the weariness we often feel.

How do we get that hope and keep it alive? Through prayer and worship. We must develop and nurture the habits of prayer, of relationship with God, of reflection on the scriptures. For it is out of that relationship that the vision of the day of the Lord will become real. The old saints referred to their times of prayer as "recollection of the soul." Literally, we re-collect ourselves when we become fragmented and harried and burned out. In prayer, we pull all the scattered bits of ourselves, all the depleted energies back together and become whole again.

Martin Luther, the great reformer of the church back in the 16th century, made the comment one morning when he got out of bed that his work load that day was so heavy, that he knew he would never get it all done unless he spent three hours in prayer first. Many of us find it difficult to set aside 15 minutes a day for prayer, let alone three hours, but then, not many of us are having the impact on the world that Martin Luther did either. It was in his prayer that all his energies were collected, and his action became focused and effective.

What was true of Luther has been true of all those who have been effective and faithful servants of Christ. Who can imagine the incredible success of the early Methodist movement without the disciplined prayer life of John Wesley and the early Methodist class meetings where people gathered to pray, to worship, to encourage and exhort one another in love? Wesley once wrote to a young preacher who was suffering from burn-out, "O begin! Fix some time every day to read the scriptures and to pray. It is for your life. Without this all else would be trifling and idleness." The list could go on and on. All who have been faithful witnesses and seemingly tireless in doing what is right have been sustained and inspired by their hope in God's new creation, and for all of them, that vision has been kept alive by a regular and disciplined habit of prayer.

But it is not only our personal prayer which is essential: None of us can find sufficient strength for the work by ourselves. Faith and hope are found in community. By joining together in the corporate praise of God, in worship, we re-envision the world. In worship, we deny that money or power or violence of death rule the world, and we declare that God is the real ruler. In our liturgy, our hymns, our prayers of intercession, our listening and responding to the proclaimed word, we discover a new framework for understanding who we are and what we're about. And in this community solidarity, we discover hope and a new source of energy to overcome our world-weariness and continue doing what is right. Prayer and worship are our weapons against burn-out.

Are you feeling tired and burned out trying to always do what is right? Are you weary in well-doing? Or is your hope in God's future, nurtured in prayer and worship, sustaining you and bringing to you the power of the Spirit to enable you to be a faithful witness to Jesus Christ? The prophet Isaiah has expressed this hope and confidence perhaps more beautifully than anyone else:

> *Have you not known? Have you not heard?*
> *The Lord is the everlasting God,*
>   *the Creator of the ends of the earth.*
> *He does not faint or grow weary;*
> *He gives power to the faint,*
>   *and strengthens the powerless.*
> *Even youths will faint and be weary,*
>   *and the young will fall exhausted.*
> *But those who wait in hope for the Lord will renew*
>   *their strength.*
> *They will mount up with wings like eagles,*
> *They will run and not be weary,*
> *They will walk and not faint.*
>   — *Isaiah 40:28-31*

Pentecost 27 (L)
Luke 19:11-27

Investing God's Gift

One of the things that frequently happens when we dream during sleep is that in our dreams we find ourselves in a familiar place or situation. We know where we are, yet for some really frustrating and unknown reason, things are just different enough that we're not really sure. In our dream we're about to open a door only to discover that the door isn't where we know it ought to be. Or perhaps we're about to perform a familiar act, and somehow, we just can't do it, and we can't understand why. We keep trying and the more we try the more frustrated we become. Sometimes the frustration becomes so great that we even wake up.

Reading this story from Luke's gospel has something of that same familiar and yet strange quality. We know it, or it feels like we do, and yet, as we read it, we're not quite sure that we do know it after all. There are some perplexing and troubling features that make us take a second look. Is this really the story as we remember it? Weren't there three servants instead of ten? Weren't they given talents instead of pounds? (After all, we usually speak of "the Parable of the Talents.") And we don't remember anybody getting slaughtered; they may be cast out into outer darkness and there is something about "weeping and wailing and gnashing of teeth." But slaughtered? That's a little extreme, isn't it?

That very strangeness cues us in to the fact that it is Matthew's version of this story which is far and away the most familiar. Luke's version is hardly ever told, and for some very understandable reasons. It's fairly perplexing and not a little disturbing. It is probably just because of the disturbing picture which Luke's story presents that we almost always quote or allude to Matthew's version of the parable of the talents rather than to Luke's. But perhaps, for that reason, we need to take a closer look at how Luke uses this familiar parable of Jesus to give it his own special twist.

Luke's version appears to be a conflation of two stories. One is a parable about a master who goes away after distributing money to some servants and charging them with investing it in his absence. The other is a story about a nobleman who went away to receive a royal commission, but who was hated and opposed by his fellow citizens, and who took revenge on them upon receiving his royal power. In all likelihood, the stories had already been linked in the oral tradition prior to Luke's use of them. The really troublesome part for many readers is precisely due to the second story about the bloody vengeance which the returning nobleman wreaks on those who oppose his rule over them. If, as is likely, we equate the nobleman with Jesus, then the story comes to its end with a terrifying vision of judgment without mercy or quarter given. Nor is the judgment proportional to the crime. The crime was political dissent: "We do not want this man to rule over us." Hardly reason for the nobleman's sentence of doom: "As for these enemies of mine who did not want me to be king over them — bring them here and slaughter them in my presence." Can we really imagine Jesus doing such a thing?

It would be tempting to simply separate those two conflated stories from each other, think about the parable of the servants who are given a sum of money to invest in their lord's absence, which is the familiar part, the part we think we know, and forget about the violent and harsh story of the slaughtered dissenters. In fact, that's what is usually done. Even the commentators do little more than identify the two stories that have been conflated; most go on to comment on the parable of the hoarded gifts and make no attempt to interpret the other. Yet, if Luke's gospel is Holy Scripture, we cannot look away quite so quickly. Nor are we justified in simply treating each story separately. Luke has used this material with great care and it is by paying attention to how he has used it that we may come to understand some of the meanings.

The story of the nobleman who went away to receive a royal commission may have been inspired by an actual event. After the death of Herod the Great, his son Archelaus travelled to Rome to petition the emperor to be made king over Judea in his father's place. A delegation of some 50 citizens of Judea followed him to lodge their protests against this proposal, since the rule of Herod was so brutal, and they didn't want to take any chances with his son. Though there is no evidence that Archelaus had his opponents slaughtered after successfully gaining his royal commission, it would not have been at all out of character for him to have done so, given what we are able to discern of his character and method of governing. Certainly the notion of a king carrying out such vengeance upon his opponents would not have shocked the sensibilities of people in Luke's day.

I'm not sure it really shocks our sensibilities as much as we might claim. After living through or reading about Stalin's purges of all those suspected of opposing him, or the Chinese government's brutal treatment of dissidents at Tienanmen Square, or even the more humane, but no less decisive, political purges that take place in our country when a new Administration comes to power, we've grown accustomed to such patterns of "royal" behavior. We even give those bloodless purges gruesome names like "The Saturday Night Massacre" or "The Night of the Long Knives." I'm not sure human nature is all that much different now from what it was in Luke's day.

Very possibly, when this part of the story was first told, it may have been told as a polemical allegory against those Jews who had refused to accept Jesus as the Messiah. In this reading of it, Jesus would have been the nobleman who went to receive a royal commission. And the harsh judgment which fell on those of his own fellow citizens who rejected him would have been richly deserved. And in light of the devastating war that ravaged Judea after Jesus' crucifixion, culminating in the destruction of the temple in A.D. 70, along with the slaughter of thousands of the inhabitants of Jerusalem, it would have been perfectly natural to see that devastation as the judgment that fell upon those in Israel who refused to accept Jesus as their Messiah.

Yet those events were several decades in the past by the time Luke wrote his gospel, so it seems unlikely that this is still, for him, a religious polemic against the Jewish religious leaders who had rejected Jesus. Luke himself has provided us with the clues to what this story means for him in the introduction which he composed himself. The first clue is in the opening line, "As they were listening to this . . ." Listening to what? To the story of Zacchaeus which immediately precedes this one. In that story, Jesus graciously overrides all the social stigma which covers Zacchaeus and graciously invites Zacchaeus to be his host. Zacchaeus repents eagerly, and Jesus announces that salvation has come to this social pariah because the Son of Man has come to seek and to save the lost. So wherever else our passage today may lead us, it cannot be separated from the story which precedes it, the story of a Savior who seeks out the lowest, the most despised, and even the wicked tax collectors like Zacchaeus. The parable which follows comes "as they were listening" to the story of Zacchaeus.

The second clue Luke gives us is the latter part of that introductory sentence: "He went on to tell a parable because he was near Jerusalem, and because they supposed that the kingdom of God was to appear immediately." Though there is ample evidence, both in the New Testament itself as well as in other early Christian writings, that the earliest Christians expected Christ to return shortly after his resurrection, as time went on and the end didn't come, the church had to come to terms with the possibility that the interval between resurrection and second coming might be prolonged. How can Luke begin to communicate the nature of that prolonged interval to his own community and help them understand how they are to live? That's his task. And this parable plays a large role in his purpose.

The parable of the investments is a parable that urges responsible mission during the time of the Lord's absence. That the nobleman intends to return is clear: He explicitly says that he will return. Luke is not giving up the notion of Christ's return in glory to establish the full expression of the kingdom. But neither is he favorable to the inaction or lack of zeal for the mission of the church on the part of those who expect that return imminently. The point is, no one knows when the nobleman will return. No one knows how long his journey will delay his homecoming. In the meantime, there is work to be done, money to be invested, profits to be made. The ten servants who are each given a pound (or approximately three-months worth of wages for a daily laborer) are charged equitably. None is given a heavier responsibility than the others. Yet neither is less expected from them than that they shall be faithful to the charge to the limits of their individual abilities.

When the nobleman does return, he does not upbraid those servants who reaped lesser profits as long as they conscientiously and faithfully attempted to follow their master's instructions. All those who followed the master's instructions and returned to him, not only his original investment, but the profits they had earned with it, are rewarded.

He does have harsh words, however, for the one servant who either from fear or indolence, failed to follow the master's instructions. His self-justifying rationalization for hoarding the money given to him by the master meets with sharp and swift discipline. The hoarded gift is taken away from him and given to the one who had reaped the largest profit from the money entrusted to him.

A friend who lived for a time in East Malaysia told of a story that appeared in the newspaper one day and shocked the city. A well-known beggar had died. He had been part of the landscape of that city for many years. Each day, those who stopped at the food stalls near the bus station would be sure to see this man. He would approach their table, but not too closely to be obtrusive. He would hold out his hand and stand there silently for a minute or two. If those from whom he was begging did not respond within that time, he would move on to the next table and repeat his performance. Everyone in town knew where he slept at night. He slept on the veranda of one of the Chinese temples in town. Since the weather was warm year-round, he only needed the roof of the veranda for shelter from the rain. Worshippers who came to the temple would often give alms to him as an act of merit before going into the temple to pray.

It wasn't his death that shocked everyone; he was getting on in years, and his way of life could not have been conducive to long life. The shock came when it was discovered that he had over $40,000 in the knapsack he always carried around with him. Even more amazing was the fact that he had made a will and left all his money to the temple where he had slept all those years.

All that money gained from years of begging, and yet it did him no good whatsoever. He could have had better clothing. He could have paid for his own meals. He could have rented a room. He might even have married and started a family. Instead he dressed in rags, he lived on the streets, and he survived on handouts and food scraps, all the while accumulating his bankroll of money in his knapsack. It did neither him nor anyone else any good at all.

Luke's message is clear: The gift which the church has received is the gift of salvation through Jesus Christ. Yet it is a gift that carries with it the charge to invest it and make it grow. The time of the Lord's absence is the time for mission, not for hoarding the gift. The servants who are entrusted with their master's money are to act on his behalf. They are to invest as though the master himself was investing. And so it is with the salvation which God has effected through the death and resurrection of Jesus Christ. Those to whom that message has been entrusted are accountable for seeing that it gets invested properly. Neither a too intense expectation of the Lord's return, nor a lazy, indifferent attitude will suffice. Both will be judged. The proper posture for the church to adopt in this indefinite time of the Lord's absence is faithfulness to the task it has been given. It is not the time of the return that is important; rather the important thing is faithfulness to the mission.

This is a message that many modern Christians may not want to hear. Evangelism, witnessing, testifying — these are not terms frequently heard, at least in "mainline" churches these days. We tend to think about which of our own needs we expect the church to meet, rather than thinking about the needs outside the church which we can meet. In our cultural atmosphere of religious pluralism and moral relativism, we're not sure if it's even desirable or acceptable to stand for something, much less to proclaim it with the intent of drawing others into our fellowship. Yet the question is inescapable. What has been entrusted to us? And to what end? Is there salvation for the world in Jesus Christ, and if so, how will that become known? Paul asked the same question in his epistle to the Romans, "How shall they believe in one of whom they have never heard, and how shall they hear without someone to proclaim him?" How indeed, unless those to whom the message has been entrusted stop hoarding the gift and begin to invest themselves in the task they've been given.

So if this part of Luke's conflated parable is his answer to those whom he described in his introductory statement as supposing "that the kingdom of God was to appear immediately," we are still left with the other part of the story — the vengeful nobleman and his bloody retribution on those who oppose his rule over them. What are we to make of that? It doesn't even square with the actions of the master toward the servant who had failed to invest the money committed to his charge. Even there, in the case of clear negligence and disobedience, the master merely stripped the servant of his privileges; he didn't cut off his head or have him tortured. Yet in the next breath, it would seem, he orders the slaughter of those who were his political opponents.

I suggest that only by paying attention to the larger context of this story do we see the lines of Luke's thinking and his own understanding of this troubling double story. The fact that it occurs immediately after the Zacchaeus story with its emphasis on the "wideness in God's mercy" is a point which cannot be overemphasized. But even more telling is what follows it. For what follows is not the account of a king who received royal power and lords it over his subjects, brutally suppressing dissent and slaughtering his opponents. Rather, Jesus' journey into Jerusalem, the place where he is to receive royal power, or so his disciples presume, culminates in his own slaughter. Far from being the kind of king who acts as kings have always acted — as little tin gods — this king reigns from his cross. And so, being quick to see the tragic irony in this story, by his skillful placing of it in this context, Luke highlights the stark contrast between the kind of king the nobleman in the story is and the kind of king Jesus actually is. Coming from the lips of Jesus himself, this story of a murderous king is followed by his own living out of a completely different model of royal authority and power.

So if this time is the time for faithful and zealous mission, Luke is saying, it is also a time for faithfully bearing witness to a king who exercises his royal power by dying for his enemies rather than by slaughtering them after the fashion of earthly kings. To look for a kingdom that mimics the kingdom of imperial Rome or any other earthly kingdom is to look for the wrong thing. The kingdom that is coming, and which has already appeared in the salvation of a sinner like Zacchaeus, is a kingdom that demands both to be proclaimed with the utmost diligence and zeal and to be modelled with the highest expression of self-giving love. If God will hold us accountable for our faithfulness in investing the gospel with which we have been entrusted, God will also expect that we will carry out that charge following the example of the One who came "to seek and to save the lost," even at the cost of his own life.

Holding these two responsibilities in a dynamic tension is not easy. Zealous proclamation of the gospel can easily slip into zealotism — an exclusivist attitude of superiority. The intolerance of those on the religious right who appear to want to establish a theocracy smacks of such zealotism. But so does the intolerance of the religious left which appears to have elevated "inclusiveness" as the central doctrine of Christian faith and which militantly excludes anyone unenlightened enough to conform. Balance is essential. And the only thing that can enable us to maintain that balance is to follow the model we have been given — the model of a king whose symbol of victory over his enemies was an old rugged cross. If we can be faithful and zealous in our mission, while at the same time modelling the wideness of God's mercy in our conduct, then we too will hear the king say at his return, "Well done, good and faithful servant."

Thanksgiving Day
John 6:25-35 (C)
Luke 17:11-19 (L, RC)

The Bread That Endures

Perhaps you did something this morning that many others do each morning as well — you had a piece of toast or a bagel for breakfast. Perhaps you put strawberry jam or honey on your toast and spread some cream cheese on your bagel. Around the world, this simple human ritual is repeated in a variety of ways. In Malaysia, that same piece of toast might be smeared with *kaya*, a thick jam made from coconut milk. In Taiwan or in Beijing, instead of toast, it may be a steamed bun filled with bits of roast pork and vegetables. In India, the morning ritual includes rolling out some simple whole wheat dough into flat round chapatis. In France, those wonderful flaky croissants will tantalize many palates first thing in the morning. The old saying about bread being the "staff of life" is not merely a cliché. It's true. There's probably no more universal food than bread. Since human beings first learned to cultivate grains, they have been grinding that grain into flour or meal and baking bread.

Perhaps that's why baking bread is such a satisfying activity. Not only is the aroma of baking bread one of life's great olfactory pleasures, but baking bread is an activity that is fundamental to human life, and doing it links us with something very basic. Perhaps if we could get the leaders of the various warring communities together in a kitchen to bake bread, some of the prejudices and ancient animosities which result in so much violence would be dissipated. It's hard to think violent thoughts when your arms are elbow-deep in flour.

It's little wonder then that bread has become a metaphor for life itself. Not only in English, but in many languages, bread symbolizes life. So we don't need to strain our minds too hard to understand what Jesus means when he says, in our gospel lesson, "I am the Bread of Life. Whoever comes to me will never be hungry and whoever believes in me will never be thirsty." We know immediately what he means. And perhaps just because his meaning is so clear, we skip right over it without giving it much thought. Hardly any statement in the Bible is more transparently obvious. And yet, as John shows us, those to whom that statement was spoken didn't understand it nearly so readily. Perhaps its meaning is not quite as transparent as it seems at first glance, or perhaps one has to be in a certain condition in order to understand it.

The obvious meaning of Jesus' words are that, like bread, he is the one who gives and sustains life. He nourishes the eater. Just as physical bread sustains the life of the body, so Jesus sustains the life of the spirit. To come to Jesus or to believe in him is to live life as it was meant to be lived, to know life in its richest and fullest sense.

Yet so many people seem to miss out on life in that full and rich sense. Why? Possibly it's because so many have a distorted understanding of bread. If Jesus uses bread as a metaphor for the deeper dimensions of life, we have often done just the reverse. In our colloquial speech, bread does not refer to the deeper aspects of life, but to material things, specifically to money. When the teenager comes to his father and says, "Dad, I need some bread," he's not asking for his dad's wise counsel. He's not even asking for a peanut butter and jelly sandwich. When we see someone whiz by us in a new BMW, we say, "Wouldn't it be nice to have the bread for one of those?" Our figures of speech betray our understanding of reality and our true values. For us the staff of life is money. Money is what makes life both possible and worth living. We have twisted the philosopher Descarte's statement, "I think; therefore I am," into "I buy; therefore I am."

We're not the first people in history to confuse our metaphors and therefore, confuse our values. The prophet Isaiah chided the people of Israel, "Why do you spend your money for that which is not bread, and your labor for that which does not satisfy?" (Isaiah 55:2). And in our passage today, we hear Jesus saying to his disciples, "Do not work for the bread which perishes, but for the bread which endures to eternal life." There has always been a temptation for people to think that material things and physical reality are the only things that are real. It's so much easier to concentrate on what we can see and touch than it is to deal with the more intangible, though no less real, aspects of life. It's easier to surround ourselves with gadgets and gizmos that make noise and entertain us than it is to take the journey inward to silence and solitude where we meet God at the center of our beings. We do spend our substance on that which is not really bread and labor for that which does not really satisfy.

The strange thing is that, deep down inside, we really know that focussing on material things does not really satisfy the sharpest hungers of our souls. Not many of us are under the illusion that our deepest yearnings can be satisfied by the things we buy. We know instinctively and intuitively that when Jesus says "One does not live by bread alone, but by every word which comes from the mouth of God," he is absolutely correct. We know, too, that Frederick Buechner is correct when he writes that when we eat bread we acknowledge our dependence, not only on food for our physical life, but on God and on others, for the emptiness of our bellies reminds us of other kinds of emptiness which not even the blue plate special can fill.

And yet, almost as though we can't help ourselves, we keep striving to get more and more material things, more and more money, *as though* those things could fill up the spiritual and emotional hungers of our souls. We neglect the life of the spirit, we avoid prayer, we avoid intimacy with others, we run away from ourselves, from God, from the living Bread which gives eternal life.

If one danger is that we ignore our need for spiritual bread in favor of the bread which does not satisfy, another related, and equally deadly, danger is that we try to satisfy both our material and spiritual hungers, but keep them completely separate from each other. It is very easy for us to break our life into little compartments. In one compartment we keep our job. Whatever we do at work, whatever decisions we have to make, the language we use in the office or shop floor, stays in that little box labelled work. In another compartment we have our pleasures. And we pursue these as though they are unrelated to anything else in our lives. Another compartment is labelled home and family, and we behave in certain ways that may be very different from the way we behave at work or at the football stadium. A fourth compartment is labelled religion or church, and we're a different person there too. We give God a certain portion of ourselves, our time, our money, and our energies. But we keep God confined within that box labelled religion. We don't allow God to get in the box labelled job or pleasure or family. We "have" our religion the same way that we "have" season tickets to the New York Giants games or a new Toyota.

This ability to compartmentalize our lives leads inevitably to the absurd situation where people who claim to be good Christians can surround themselves with every material comfort money can buy and, at the same time, feel little or no responsibility for their homeless neighbors on the streets of their city or for their neighbors dying of starvation in the Sudan, or even for their hurting neighbor across the street who's just gone through a painful divorce or is struggling with a life-threatening illness. Oh, to be sure, we sometimes feel compassion, and even sometimes give money to various world hunger projects or other worthy causes. But we don't really ever get to the point of breaking down the walls between the compartments in our lives in order to see that our confession of Christ is the center which organizes and controls every aspect of our lives, whether it be our life at work or at home or at play. By keeping all the compartments separate, we can be as spiritual as we want to be, but our spirituality will be a private and personal thing without any necessary connection to any other area of our lives.

But as Jesus' statements about bread make clear, our physical or material life and our spiritual life are inseparable. Any attempt to separate them results in a distortion. Much of the meaning of our sacrament of holy communion is to be found just at this point. We are reminded graphically of the wholeness of our lives, of how deeply dependent we are for both spiritual and physical life upon the grace of God in Jesus Christ. The bread which we eat at the Lord's table is real bread. It's flour and water and salt. It reminds us of the basic necessity of food for our bodies. Eating bread ties us intimately to all other human beings for whom bread is the staff of life. It also reminds us that in Jesus Christ, God took on real flesh and blood, thereby forever sanctifying the material world. At the same time, this bread of the sacrament also has a transcendent meaning. It conveys to us the very presence of Christ himself. It is Christ's body. He is our bread. His life is meditated to us so that our life transcends the merely physical and begins to partake of that quality of life which belongs to God — eternal life.

Mortimer Arias, a Methodist bishop in Bolivia, tells a story which graphically brings home to us the meaning of the bread of life. He was at a worship service in a rural area of the country, but there was no church building. The service was being held in a large tent. Bishop Arias was celebrating the sacrament of the Lord's supper. Among the crowd of people coming to the front to receive the elements, he noticed a barefoot boy about 11 years old. When the plate with the tiny pieces of bread passed in front of him, instead of taking one piece as is customary, he began grabbing whole handfuls of bread and eating it hungrily. It was then that Bishop Arias realized that this little boy from this poor area of Bolivia really was hungry. For him the bread at communion was not just a spiritual symbol. It was, in reality, the staff of life. The bishop said that he suddenly understood the sacrament of the Lord's supper in an entirely new way. He understood God's intention for the wholeness and connectedness of life.

When we recover that sense of the wholeness and integration of both spiritual and material aspects of life, we will be able to celebrate Thanksgiving in a much deeper way. Our feasting on the stuffed turkey and all the fixings of our traditional dinner will not be simply another orgy of over-eating, but a reminder of how deeply dependent we are on the Bread of Heaven for life itself, and of how deeply connected we are with every other person, and particularly those for whom bread is a luxury. When we begin to allow the hungers of our bellies and the hungers of our souls to be integrated, then we will discover a connection to the compassion of God that will enable us to become broken bread and poured out wine for others, that they too might find the Bread of Life.

Christ The King
Luke 23:33-43 (C)
Luke 23:35-43

Pleased To Reconcile

Did you ever secretly wish that we had kings and queens here in America? I think that must be a secret wish of many of us, if the tabloid newspapers and magazines which are always on sale at the supermarket checkout counters are any indication. Between the romantic antics of Hollywood and the goings-on of the British royal family, the tabloids do a rushing business. (I won't embarrass any of us by asking how many secretly enjoy reading those tabloids as we're standing in line.) There's hardly a week goes by that there isn't some story about the latest marital couplings among the British royals. From all appearances, poor Queen Elizabeth, like her illustrious and straitlaced grandmother, Queen Victoria, is definitely not amused. Personally, I think the British royal family is worth every penny they're paid for the service they perform in keeping the media, and therefore the public attention, focussed on them, leaving the government free to get on with its business. Although it's unlikely we'll get a royal family for ourselves, we do seem to be in love with the idea of royalty.

Today is the last Sunday in the Christian year, the Sunday we call Christ the King. It's fitting to conclude the liturgical year with an acclamation of the royalty of Christ, though we do this much more frequently than once a year. The sovereignty of Christ is well-affirmed in our hymns and in the language we use to speak about Jesus in our worship. In a few weeks, we'll be singing "Come and worship, come and worship, worship Christ the newborn king," and "Hark! the herald angels sing, glory to the newborn king," as we celebrate Christmas.

But as often as we use the language of royalty in our praise of Christ, I wonder if we really have a good understanding of what we mean when we hail Jesus as a king, and what, if anything, the kingship of Jesus has to do with our lives. Those two questions, it seems to me, are ones we have to consider seriously: What does it mean to confess Jesus as King, and what personal significance does that confession have for us?

Both our epistle and gospel lessons refer to Jesus as king. In the gospel lesson, the term is overlaid with heavy irony. It is Jesus' executioners, the Roman soldiers, who use the term in their mocking taunt: "If you are the King of the Jews, save yourself." The clear implication is that if Jesus is a king, then kingship doesn't mean much. Even the inscription written over his head, "This is the King of the Jews," is clearly meant as a final insult to this one who wears a crown, not of gold and precious gems, but of thorns, and whose throne is not a stately seat of power, but a rough wooden cross on which he is hung up to die. So much for all would-be royal pretenders!

Yet Luke paints for us a portrait of one who, even as he is dying, and even as he is cruelly mocked by the perverse titles and trappings of royalty, nevertheless acts like a king in his dying moments. One of the criminals who has been crucified with him suddenly is overcome by remorse and a keen feeling that this man on the next cross is a victim of cruel injustice, while he is getting no more than he deserves, and in his own agony, he says, "Jesus, remember me when you come into your kingdom." And Jesus replies with the calm authority of a true king, "Truly I tell you, today you will be with me in Paradise."

If we leave this narrative of Jesus' crucifixion with its ironic mockery, and turn to the epistle passage from Colossians, we find what appears to be a hymn-like paean of praise to Christ which employs some of the most exalted language in the

New Testament. This truly is praise for a king, and not the ironic taunts of enemies or executioners. Listen to the phrases: "the image of the invisible God, the firstborn of all creation ... the head of the body, the church, the firstborn from the dead ... in him all the fullness of God was pleased to dwell" (Colossians 1:15, 18-19). That's language fit for royalty, isn't it? This is more like it, we think. This is language we can sink our teeth into and take pride in. We who are followers of Jesus can relate to language like this.

Unfortunately, down through the centuries, the church has often let these magnificent cadences of praise lead it into triumphalism. In the name of Christ the King, or the Pantocrator as he was called in the early church (meaning "Ruler of the Universe"), the church militant has often trampled its enemies, conquered and converted people by the sword, and imposed both spiritual and temporal rule over people through the use of terror.

And yet, it is not these wonderful praises from Colossians which are to be blamed; rather it is the church's failure to read them closely enough. For the author has not contented himself with this majestic and exalted praise of Christ. He has not left the door open to the kind of triumphalism to which Christians have often succumbed. He has clearly anchored these praises to the concrete event of Jesus' death on the cross. "Through him, God was pleased to reconcile all things, whether on earth or in heaven, by making peace through the blood of his cross" (Colossians 1:20). This is the sentence that qualifies and defines the meaning of all those high-sounding praises. This is the sentence that illuminates what it means to be the image of the invisible God, the firstborn of all creation, and so on. The majestic and glorious king of heaven is none other than the one who "made peace through the blood of his cross."

What Luke has done narratively to show us what kind of a king Jesus is, the author of Colossians has done theologically. Luke shows us a dying Jesus reconciling a penitent criminal. The writer of Colossians shows us the God whose saving plan to reconcile all things in earth and heaven stands behind, and is carried out through, that same dying Jesus.

If history did not tell the story, who would believe that, nearly 2,000 years after an obscure Galilean peasant, who gained some local notoriety as a wandering preacher and healer, and was executed by the Romans who were very touchy about any perceived threat to their imperial domination, there would not be a single nation in the world where this obscure peasant was not worshipped and acclaimed as a king, a king whose kingdom shall never end, and who by his power holds the universe together? Fantastic, isn't it! Where in this world can one go and not discover somewhere a group of people who confess Jesus as Lord and King? In countries rich and poor, large and small, with repressive or democratic governments, the church which Christ has gathered into one body, and of which he is the head, is present and growing.

In the highlands of the interior of the East Malaysian state of Sarawak on the heavily-forested island of Borneo, there is a small village called Barrio. It is only accessible by small planes capable of landing on the tiny mountain-ringed runway, or by a long journey by canoes up jungle rivers and trekking on foot. And yet, every person in that village confesses the Lordship of Jesus Christ. In southern Zaire, where political turmoil and corrupt government has many people on the brink of starvation, there are small groups of Christians who gather in rural mud-brick churches, sometimes without even a roof, and there each Sunday, they sing the praises of a king whose name is Jesus. Through the long years of repression in the Soviet Union and its satellites, and in China where for so many years public worship was forbidden, we now discover in this era when the walls of repression are falling that the church was not only alive but growing, and is now stronger than it ever was in those lands. Many people in those lands refused to confess Mao Tse-Tung or Stalin or Brezhnev as king, preferring to confess Jesus as king instead, sometimes at great personal cost.

Somehow, that historical development — the universal reign of One who died as a subversive criminal at the town dump of Jerusalem nearly 2,000 years ago — must be explained. It certainly cannot be explained by the misguided attempts of the church to impose that rule by force or intimidation down through the centuries. All those attempts have ended in ruinous failure. Nor was it merely the power of the ideas which Jesus proclaimed, though those ideas are powerful, and have undoubtedly shaped lives and nations. Something more is at work here.

In his marvelous series of children's books called *The Chronicles of Narnia*, C. S. Lewis tells stories of the imaginary land of Narnia and the king who rules it, a king whose name is Aslan. Aslan is a lion, the Great Lion, at whose roar the very trees of the forest tremble in awe.

In the first book of the series, four human children are playing in an old wardrobe when they suddenly discover that it is a doorway to Narnia. Narnia, at this junction in its history, is under the spell of a wicked witch whose rule is evil and oppressive. The youngest child, Lucy, gives the best description of Narnia under the witch's rule: "It's always winter, but never Christmas." The children enter into a plot to overthrow the power of the witch, since they hear from some of the inhabitants a rumor that Aslan the rightful king is returning. One of the children, however, the younger boy Edmund, is a spoiled brat, and when he discovers that he can't have everything his way, he betrays the other animals and his brother and sisters to the witch, and they fall into her clutches.

In the climactic scene, the witch comes to Aslan and tells him that according to the deep magic from the dawn of time, she is entitled to have the blood of anyone who is a traitor. So she demands to be allowed to sacrifice Edmund on the Stone Table, a large ritual stone that has always been in Narnia. Aslan acknowledges the justice of her claim, but then offers to become the victim of the sacrifice himself in place of Edmund.

The witch, of course, is delighted at this offer, for she not only gets the blood she demands, but gets rid of her ancient enemy and arch-rival Aslan at the same time. Before the horrified eyes of the children, Aslan allows himself to be bound, humiliated, and slaughtered on the Stone Table to the triumphant howls of the witch. The two girls Susan and Lucy stay all night by his body, grieving their loss, for now it is obvious the wicked witch has won, and her rule over Narnia will be secure.

But at sunrise, when they walk away a short distance to stretch their legs, they suddenly hear a gigantic crack, and when they look around, the Stone Table is split from end to end and the body of Aslan is gone. Suddenly they hear his voice, and there in the morning sunlight he stands alive and more majestic than ever!

When they express their delight and their surprise, Aslan tells them that the witch knew the deep magic from the dawn of time, but that there is a deeper magic which she did not know. Her knowledge only went back to the dawn of time, he says.

> *But if she could have looked a little further back into the stillness and darkness before Time, she would have read there a different incantation. She would have known that when a willing victim who had committed no treachery is killed in a traitor's stead, the Table would crack, and Death itself would start working backward.*[1]

That's what the writer of Colossians is getting at when he mentions the blood of Jesus' cross in the same breath as the images of the exalted, cosmic Christ. That's what Luke is getting at when he tells us in story fashion of a man who in his dying agony can find it within himself to royally pronounce forgiveness and reconciliation to a penitent criminal. That old cross at the town dump of Jerusalem was, in reality, the symbol of kingly power that had its origins far back in "the deeper magic from before the dawn of time." It was the power that started death working backward. So Jesus became "the first-born from the dead," the first in a long series of men and women over whom death can never again hold ultimate power to destroy. Those who confess this dying man on the cross as king are "transferred from the kingdom of darkness to the kingdom of God's beloved Son." Those who confess him as king are people for whom the crown of thorns and the nails and the cross of shame are emblems of a royal power the likes of which the world has never seen before or since, and which is greater than the mightiest armies, the richest corporations, the most destructive thermonuclear warheads, or the most thorough political revolutions. His royal power is the power of suffering love, of sacrifice, of faith in the power of God to raise the dead, and that power is the supreme power in heaven and earth.

So, then, what does it mean to us personally to confess Jesus as king? Is it anything more than high-sounding words that we sing in hymns or affirm in our liturgy? That depends on the extent to which we commit ourselves to the lordship of Jesus. Whatever we commit ourselves to is what determines our behavior and shapes our lives. It follows then, that if we commit ourselves to Jesus as king, then the definition of kingship he lived out will determine the way we live under that kingship. If his kingship is defined by his sacrificial death for others on the cross, then our lives will be cross-shaped as well.

This means that in our relationships with other people, we take our king's way of conducting ourselves. His way was to forgive and reconcile a penitent criminal. Our way, then, can do no less than be forgiving and reconciling. His way was to give himself willingly for others; our way can do no less than be self-giving for the benefit of others as well. If our lives had sufficient value to him that he would die for us, then we must place no less value on ourselves than he did. This means, among other things, that we do not abuse our bodies with substances that are destructive, we do not abuse ourselves or others with exploitative sexual behavior. We resolve to be the best persons we can be with the help of his grace. In that way, we honor his trust in us.

If Jesus is king, he is king not only in the personal sphere of individual integrity and relationships with other people. He is king of the whole universe, and therefore, that lordship must be acknowledged and confessed in our relationships to the earth itself. We have to stop seeing ourselves as owners and begin confessing that we are stewards of the creation. So we will exercise that stewardship conscientiously, repenting of our wasteful and polluting behavior, husbanding the earth's resources instead of exploiting them for the single motive of profit.

In short, there is no area of our lives to which the king's authority does not extend. Nothing can be withheld from our confession of Jesus as Lord and king. If he is sovereign at all, he must and will be sovereign of all. And the way we live in our personal lives, our business dealings, our social and family relationships, our lives as citizens and keepers of the earth — all will testify to whose kingdom we have pledged our allegiance.

---

1. Lewis, C.S., *The Lion, The Witch And The Wardrobe*, (Collier Books: New York, New York, 1970), p. 160.

Lectionary Preaching After Pentecost

Virtually all pastors who make use of the sermons in this book will find their worship life and planning shaped by one of two lectionary series. Most mainline Protestant denominations, along with clergy of the Roman Catholic Church, have now approved — either for provisional or official use — the three-year Revised Common (Consensus) Lectionary. This family of denominations includes United Methodist, Presbyterian, United Church of Christ and Disciples of Christ.

Lutherans and Roman Catholics, while testing the Revised Common Lectionary on a limited basis at present, follow their own three-year cycle of texts. While there are divergences between the Revised Common and Lutheran/Roman Catholic systems, the gospel texts show striking parallels, with few text selections evidencing significant differences. Nearly all the gospel texts included in this book will, therefore, be applicable to worship and preaching planning for clergy following either lectionary.

A significant divergence does occur, however, in the method by which specific gospel texts are assigned to specific calendar days. The Revised Common and Roman Catholic Lectionaries accomplish this by counting backwards from Christ the King (Last Sunday after Pentecost), discarding "extra" texts from the front of the list: Lutherans follow the opposite pattern, counting forward from The Holy Trinity, discarding "extra" texts at the end of the list.

The following index will aid the user of this book in matching the correct text to the correct Sunday during the Pentecost portion of the church year.

(Fixed dates do not pertain to Lutheran Lectionary)

Fixed Date Lectionaries *Revised Common and Roman Catholic*	Lutheran Lectionary *Lutheran*
The Day of Pentecost	The Day of Pentecost
The Holy Trinity	The Holy Trinity
May 29-June 4 — Proper 4, Ordinary Time 9	Pentecost 2
June 5-11 — Proper 5, Ordinary Time 10	Pentecost 3
June 12-18 — Proper 6, Ordinary Time 11	Pentecost 4
June 19-25 — Proper 7, Ordinary Time 12	Pentecost 5
June 26-July 2 — Proper 8, Ordinary Time 13	Pentecost 6

July 3-9 — Proper 9, Ordinary Time 14	Pentecost 7
July 10-16 — Proper 10, Ordinary Time 15	Pentecost 8
July 17-23 — Proper 11, Ordinary Time 16	Pentecost 9
July 24-30 — Proper 12, Ordinary Time 17	Pentecost 10
July 31-Aug. 6 — Proper 13, Ordinary Time 18	Pentecost 11
Aug. 7-13 — Proper 14, Ordinary Time 19	Pentecost 12
Aug. 14-20 — Proper 15, Ordinary Time 20	Pentecost 13
Aug. 21-27 — Proper 16, Ordinary Time 21	Pentecost 14
Aug. 28-Sept. 3 — Proper 17, Ordinary Time 22	Pentecost 15
Sept. 4-10 — Proper 18, Ordinary Time 23	Pentecost 16
Sept. 11-17 — Proper 19, Ordinary Time 24	Pentecost 17
Sept. 18-24 — Proper 20, Ordinary Time 25	Pentecost 18
Sept. 25-Oct. 1 — Proper 21, Ordinary Time 26	Pentecost 19
Oct. 2-8 — Proper 22, Ordinary Time 27	Pentecost 20
Oct. 9-15 — Proper 23, Ordinary Time 28	Pentecost 21
Oct. 16-22 — Proper 24, Ordinary Time 29	Pentecost 22
Oct. 23-29 — Proper 25, Ordinary Time 30	Pentecost 23
Oct. 30-Nov. 5 — Proper 26, Ordinary Time 31	Pentecost 24
Nov. 6-12 — Proper 27, Ordinary Time 32	Pentecost 25
Nov. 13-19 — Proper 28, Ordinary Time 33	Pentecost 26 Pentecost 27
Nov. 20-26 — Christ the King	Christ the King

Reformation Day (or last Sunday in October) is October 31 (Revised Common, Lutheran)

All Saints' Day (or first Sunday in November) is November 1 (Revised Common, Lutheran, Roman Catholic)

Books In This Cycle C Series

Gospel Set

When It Is Dark Enough
Sermons For Advent, Christmas And Epiphany
Charles H. Bayer

Walking To ... Walking With ... Walking Through
Sermons For Lent And Easter
Glenn E. Ludwig

The Divine Advocacy
Sermons For Pentecost (First Third)
Maurice A. Fetty

Troubled Journey
Sermons For Pentecost (Middle Third)
John Lynch

Extraordinary Faith For Ordinary Time
Sermons For Pentecost (Last Third)
Larry Kalajainen

First Lesson Set

The Days Are Surely Coming
Sermons For Advent, Christmas And Epiphany
Robert A. Hausman

Turning Obstacles Into Opportunities
Sermons For Lent And Easter
Rodney Thomas Smothers

Grapes Of Wrath Or Grace?
Sermons For Pentecost (First Third)
Barbara Brokhoff

Summer Fruit
Sermons For Pentecost (Middle Third)
Richard L. Sheffield

Stepping Inside The Story
Sermons For Pentecost (Last Third)
Thomas G. Rogers

www.ingramcontent.com/pod-product-compliance
Lightning Source LLC
Chambersburg PA
CBHW071719040426
42446CB00011B/2138